Talia,

Thank you so much
for your passion with
this field of helping
children and parents —

With much
appreciation,

Mark Rose

MW00947947

Preserving Family Ties

An Authoritative Guide To Understanding Divorce
and Child Custody, for Parents and Family Professionals

Mark David Roseman, Ph.D., CFLE

Family Court Mediator, Divorced Dad and Child Advocate
Founder and CEO, The Toby Center for Family Transitions, Inc

WESTBOW
PRESS°
A DIVISION OF THOMAS NELSON
& ZONDERVAN

Copyright © 2018 Mark David Roseman, Ph.D., CFLE.

All rights reserved. No part of this book may be used or reproduced by any means, graphic, electronic, or mechanical, including photocopying, recording, taping or by any information storage retrieval system without the written permission of the author except in the case of brief quotations embodied in critical articles and reviews.

WestBow Press books may be ordered through booksellers or by contacting:

WestBow Press
A Division of Thomas Nelson & Zondervan
1663 Liberty Drive
Bloomington, IN 47403
www.westbowpress.com
1 (866) 928-1240

Because of the dynamic nature of the Internet, any web addresses or links contained in this book may have changed since publication and may no longer be valid. The views expressed in this work are solely those of the author and do not necessarily reflect the views of the publisher, and the publisher hereby disclaims any responsibility for them.

Any people depicted in stock imagery provided by Thinkstock are models, and such images are being used for illustrative purposes only.
Certain stock imagery © Thinkstock.

ISBN: 978-1-9736-0953-7 (sc)
ISBN: 978-1-9736-0952-0 (hc)
ISBN: 978-1-9736-0954-4 (e)

Library of Congress Control Number: 2017919044

Print information available on the last page.

WestBow Press rev. date: 1/30/2018

DEDICATION

For Allison Beth, Stefanie Jill, and Andrew Scott

Always my children

For Toby and Sid, Mom and Dad

Thank you for giving me life, love, and spirit.
Without words, my love always.

For David L. Levy, Esq.

A kinder, wiser, more compassionate, dedicated, humble and
gregarious, child advocate and mentor will not easily be found.

"What children do at home, they will do to society."

—Karl Augustus Menninger, MD
The Crime of Punishment (New York: Viking Press, 1968)

CONTENTS

PART III: THE CHILD CUSTODY JOURNEY

FOREWORD

For almost 50 years, I have invested in my career of exploring mental health phenomenon and those diagnoses associated with trying to identify the entities and processes associated with the treatment of these wonders of creative minds at work. My teaching at various institutions of higher learning with my being an associate professor of psychiatry at Brown and Columbia Universities' Medical Schools and being a full professor of psychiatry at the University of Pennsylvania Medical School after receiving my post-doctorate education in the department of psychiatry at Harvard Medical School afforded me the experience of finding that medical students, psychology interns and psychiatric residents as well as practitioners in the field knew very little of what keeps us going in the true dynamic sense and puzzled workings of marriage and family processes. Couples plotted along while raising families and the children survived through development and parental conflicts. However, wounded parents and their battered children had lifelong scars of getting through this maze of uncharted territory for them. What was clear is the evidence of experienced outcomes showed individuals and partners in prior intimate relationships accumulated battle scars from their efforts to swim ashore to rescue the children they purported to love in shouting the message of trying to save them. Dr. Roseman points out his treatise of discoveries of what has happened to many of these families in an effort to appreciate and understand them and what occurs at the final point of their custody contest in their local court of jurisdiction.

For generations, women or mothers have relied upon receiving sole custody while fathers got destroyed in their attempts to bring out the darker side of some of these women whom have chosen to lie and misrepresent their former husbands and fathers in the raising of the children. Now in contemporary society, it is not necessarily a given that women receive custody but instead there is a presumption of joint custody and that the law states that these parents should continue in shared parenting even though they have chosen a different path for their own individual lives and future relationships. David Levy, an attorney and as a parents' rights advocate lead the charge and challenge by establishing a Children Rights' Council located in Washington, D.C. alongside of Dr. Roseman as his assistant in every move that he motioned the public and professional associations and practitioners of law and mental health staff in proceeding along the lines that he created.

Dr. Roseman engenders to emphasize the importance of recognizing the multiple threads of variables that appear regardless of orientation such as culture, gender and sexism, heritage, psychopathology, parental intellectual capacity, physical abilities, addictions and various displays of substance abuse, and finally psychological states that the parents present. Dr. Richard Gardner at Columbia described parental alienation syndrome where the parent went to great lengths to point out the shortcomings of one parent while blowing their own horn as being of utmost capability.

Thus, one parent was described as all competent while the other parent was referenced as all incompetent with a trail of negative findings that were spurious and found to be untrue as confabulated and constructed by the parent alienator but offered to the court as fact and real. I met Dr. Gardner at the Children's Rights Council's Annual Conference in Washington. D.C. in which they each gave book reviews: Dr. Gardner spoke of his textbook called "The Parental Alienation Syndrome" whereas I presented the book I had just written with attorney Lenard Marlow "The Handbook of Divorce Mediation" published by Plenum in NYC. This led to a close professional relationship allowing us to work together in future projects.

The child internalized what the alienator purported from the chorus of supporters which was fiction but the child believed every word which was echoed about how terrible the other parent was in which they eventually believed it or the child went along with it to be co-opted by the powerful parent that had the presence of the child within his home and network to control.

Dr. Roseman also points out that Dr. Urie Bronfenbrenner at the University of Rochester contributed his psychological-social model of what the connection was and the interplay between what we feel, what we perceive as the reality, and what we do in terms of action. This approach served as the basis for family dynamics regardless of theoretical orientation. Add to the legal terminology that has changed in the last few centuries and we have a mountain of literature which this textbook helps explain as the developing occurrences that have taken place and fathers, in particular, have gained increasing viability in the courtroom and outside of the courtroom to influence child custody and shared parenting for the children and the family. David Levy was the "king" of Joint custody as he was known to be and advocated this stance is his work and his testimony to the family courts and judges. He assisted in molding and facilitating this model whenever possible and he indirectly accomplished the task of the fathers' rights representative to further promulgating this advocacy position. This influence helped equalize the advantage that mothers had in the courts and their historical roots of taking care of the children while men engaged in income producing activities .Internationally, this trend was flourishing throughout the world as men became "fathers" and nurturing studies showed that fathers as well as mothers could play a role in child development and caring for the children, regardless of the gender. Dr. Ron Levant was considered the mover of this direction and point of view in emphasizing the importance of fathers in the family which somehow was a neglected area of study and practicality. Dr. Roseman joined David Levy in 1999 as the spokesman of joint custody and shared parenting. Dr. Roseman was speaking in NYC while Mr. Levy was speaking in Washington, D.C and through the channels he opened at the Children Rights Council which was broadcasted throughout the U.S,Canada, Europe and Australia and many locations abroad. Dr. Roseman expounds how 15 states are still struggling with the concepts of parental alienation, parental conflicts and unequal parental rights as they have become to be known for this lack of remedy and progressive approach to these new doctrines and child custody laws and statues that have been adopted in other states.

Dr. Richard Sauber
March, 2017

S. Richard Sauber, PhD, ABPP — Forensic Psychologist, is a Board-Certified Diplomate in Clinical and Family Psychology and has testified in 16 states and 17 counties within the State of Florida. He was Professor of Psychology in the Departments of Psychiatry at Brown, Columbia and the University of Pennsylvania Medical Schools in addition to being a fellow at the Harvard Medical School and the author of 16 textbooks published in the field. Dr. Sauber holds Diplomates in the American Board of Disability Consultants and the American Board of Sexology where he also maintains the status of Supervisor of New Diplomates in Training.

Dr. Sauber is Founding Editor of The American Journal of Family Therapy (1976-2015) and recommended Dr. Len Sperry, (MD and PhD) to continue in this capacity as editor. He is editor of the International Handbook of Parental Alienation Syndrome with Dr. Richard Gardner, co-editor of PARENTAL ALIENATION: The Handbook for Mental Health and Legal Professionals, and co-editor with Dr. Amy Baker of WORKING WITH ALIENATED CHILDREN AND FAMILIES

PREFACE

Thank you for picking up this book.

If a separated parent, you've taken a courageous step, perhaps one of your most difficult and initial steps in learning who and why a love relationship has markedly changed. It is an imperative to accept these changes in order to move forward emotionally and practically.

If a family professional, an attorney, a family judge, an educator, a therapist, one whose work directly affects parents and children, you will hopefully gain a new perspective of contemporary family issues that are not expressed well in the courts, or by state statute. The issues of child custody are weakly if at all acknowledged by our medical providers, clergy, or social leaders. Our public schools, its teachers, staff and management do try to assist children who are found to have severe home life issues as homelessness, poverty, mental health. Yet, they have few if any resources to offer children and parents when parents separate. The social statistics you will find later in this handbook bare them out. The cost to society is great.

My goal for each of you, my hope, is that each of you venturing now, even thumbing through those chapters whose headings may catch your eye, that each of you so doing will find a nugget, a gem, a suggestion, a statistic, a notion, a law, a discussion, something that will cause you to pause, to reflect and to use.

First written as my doctoral dissertation, *Preserving Family Ties* reflects the social science becoming more available. It, too, reveals my own discovery about marriage, about divorce, about children, about change, about surviving transitions. It is also about the social systems affecting this experience.

To be honest, I began my doctorate in family studies at the suggestion of my sister, Janet who was completing her own doctoral studies. She urged me to use the doctoral program as an alternative to my personal malaise following my divorce. Through this academic study, she advised me, I would uncover why marriages fail, how this action affects parents and children, and resources which additionally influence parental choices and child outcomes. A trained therapist, she told me the doctoral program would be personally reflective and professionally valuable. She told me I could, and should, make a difference for others. Janet opened my eyes to a new direction. My Aunt Marion encouraged me to explore every opportunity, to be open to possibilities.

Yes, I thought, I wanted to know why I internalized rejection and how self concept manifests itself as we struggle with divorce as a most difficult life change. I needed to know what I might do to help myself, to help others during the numerous divorce transitions. I sought to find some road map showing how to improve outcomes for children when parents separate.

This has proven my most perilous journey. It indeed has been my longest journey, and my most difficult, with effects lingering for years. I have often reflected on the institution of marriage where we are first attracted through love, and later, sometimes perplexed about our own conduct in the marital roles as husband, wife, and parent.

I have journeyed from fear, to serial dating, to writing and performing standup comedy. I have sometimes felt a character in a tragic comedy, with feelings heightened and disappearing as unexpected ocean waves. Yet, the journey had also inspired me to achieve academic and professional skills - all new learning - as Dr. George Olshin, my former doctoral advisor at the Union Institute & University had frequently called these wonderful, life changing experiences.

It is often the loss of a love relationship, a separation, divorce - all changes in one's most intimate social relationships, your family – which will trigger the most difficult and challenging of personal travels. This book was motivated by the search to answer the questions about my own divorce as I considered, "What has happened?" "What have I done to cause this?" "How can I go forward, as a parent, a father, and now, a single man?"

Helping me was the process of psychotherapy, and a therapist who had instructed me to consider that "the apple doesn't fall far from the tree". This was the initial epiphany for me, that the role of our own individual childhood and family experience had somehow shaped our self perspectives, and (differing) values. It was this idea that as children, we would be consciously and unconsciously subject to, influenced by, and frequently drawn to those qualities and dynamics we experienced and observed in our youth.

This was amazing to me for I then, and only then, really began to think that individuals clash more when values may be different, when traditions and cultures are not the same. But most revealing in my therapy was to especially appreciate that our lives are all about context, about who we are, as much as where we are in life, what is our emotional status, and what is the source of our belief systems. It was a moment of personal discovery to more completely accept that indeed, we are products of our early life experience. We are molded by this.

As you begin to read *Preserving Family Ties*, as your eyes scroll down the Table of Contents, as you leaf through the text, your mind will likely race. It will search for immediate answers, seeking a formula for saving yours or a client's relationships with children, husband, wife, partner. You may want a quick resolution to an already financially and emotionally draining legal separation and custody battle.

You may want to know why this has happened, to you.

You may want to know how to advise your client with more sensitivity.

You may find that help you want, for now. You are concerned for yourself, your children and/or your clients. You're concerned how to either 'navigate' the family court system or how to best prepare for a 'new' future.

It's tough, very tough to emotionally prepare for an arduous journey as well as to actively engage that journey. Whether waking in the morning to sunshine or to stormy weather, it is often our attitude, our perception, which can give us our motivation, our confidence, our support.

This book is written to help you. It provides invaluable research in family dynamics, high conflict divorce and child outcomes when parents separate, when they divorce.

It was written to offer you, the parent and you, the family practitioner, with a more complete insight as to what parents have experienced, perhaps why and how all of us in society can work towards improving the futures for parents and children post separation and divorce.

Nevertheless, this book was not written to give you a formula for action. *Preserving Family Ties* was written to provide you the context for the changes you have experienced in your marriage, your relationship, your parenting style, and your expectations. I have written this book to offer that context in which a new reality is unfolding. It is written to provide you the tools to understand the process of child custody, to apply new understandings to you or your client's case for effective co-parenting plans. This text is designed to help more fully understand the context for custody litigation. Further, it is expected the reader will find more meaningful therapeutic interventions. It was written to give you clearer meaning and purpose. It was written to help many survive this traumatic life change, divorce.

I wish to confirm for you that there is no magic wand to solve those problems that parents may encounter, real or imaginary. Our imagination can play havoc with this journey of family transition. But it's also true that the future for our children, for each parent, for grandparents and other extended family members, can be far better than imagined with information, education and support.

My goal, then, is to provide you with the background of today's society. It is also my aim to provide you with an understanding of many facets of contemporary society and to suggest that you have an opportunity to help improve outcomes for children.

Please read *Preserving Family Ties* with pen and highlighter and underline those concepts new to you, highlight sections of special interest, bookmark helpful pages. Note the plentiful research, and consider the recommendations which may offer you alternatives to more reasonable efforts to permit happier parents, and allow improved outcomes for children when parents choose to separate.

Take your time to contemplate and reflect.

Does it "take a village"? You decide; when you're ready. Meantime, please read this book carefully and with as open a mind as you can, now. It was pioneering child psychiatrist, Karl Menninger who wrote in the 1930's that as parents, we subconsciously and consciously model our values as much as our behavior serves to model for our children.

Share this book with your relatives and friends who want to help you, the parent seeking to understand the how, and why of your journey now. Share this with all those you know working in behalf of families and children, for they need to know, and understand the context in which families function, in which dysfunction may occur. All need to work in collaboration, maximizing each their own professional abilities so that, together, they will best succeed towards improving outcomes for your, our children.

Warmly,
Mark D. Roseman, Ph.D.

ACKNOWLEDGEMENTS

Preserving Family Ties has been a labor of love, frequently stressful, and always filled with the hope that it will be viewed a tool for those working with and those who are children and parents who endure high conflict in their marriage, their divorce and their separation. This book is inspired by those parents who have sought to share custody of their children in spite of obstacles as litigation and others who have made it a lifelong commitment to reunify with their children. I've met many at regional and national conferences addressing child advocacy, family law and family relations. Others I've been introduced to online, and as clients, all who have been direct, sharing their personal story in their quest for continued access to their children.

I have spent the better time of my mid life seeking understanding of my own marital life experience, its structure and function. I've spent great time in self reflection and study over many years looking for strategies to help me adjust to this tremendous loss, and seeking the possible alternatives to secure improvements in process and outcome when parents separate.

During the writing of *Preserving Family Ties*, I have had the honor of meeting many knowledgeable, self sacrificing, and forward thinking spirited individuals committed to helping me complete this project. It is for these many sacrificing individuals and program staff I wish to acknowledge.

Among those who have influenced me the most in the field of divorce and co-parenting and to whom I owe lifelong gratitude are

David L. Levy, Esq., co-founder and President of the Children's Rights Council (CRC) in Washington, DC and Alfred Ellis, empathic and kind visionary serving as Director of Child Access and Visitation for the CRC. While first hearing Dave speak at a conference on joint custody in New York City in 1999, I found his words, and his personality to resonate within me. He validated my own experience and beliefs. Here is an attorney who understood.

I couldn't wait till I could speak with him, though briefly after that conference. Then, Dave invited me to visit the CRC in Washington, which I immediately did not long afterwards. During that initial meeting, Dave asked me to assist with the next national co-parenting conference. Subsequently, I helped coordinate and manage six national conferences, frequently traveled to DC for meetings with parents and professionals from around the country who wished to change family law statutes in their states to reflect the importance of both parents in raising their children.

Dave served as my role model as a child advocate, and as a mindful leader of a service and child advocacy organization to aid families in transition. With Alfred Ellis, my dear friend and mentor in the supervised visitation process, the CRC managed nearly forty visitation centers around the country. I was honored to be asked to serve as Assistant Director of Child Access along with Margaret Wuwert of the CRC of Toledo. Al's gracious Southern demeanor and professional training skills left us when he passed from Corticobasal Degeneration, a lengthy, debilitating illness in September, 2014.

Deemed by many nationally as the "King of Joint Custody", Dave successfully appealed to the Federal Department of Health and Human Services Office of Child Support Enforcement for legislation to provide funding for mediation, supervised visitation and therapy for parents struggling in family courts (the Child Access and Visitation Block Grant). His cherubic smile, charismatic manner and frequent laughter were those qualities in leadership that were rare, but effective. Dave never had an acerbic word for anyone. He would simply raise his hands in the air, lift his eyebrows, and gave a slight smile. I revered David as a mentor; I love him as a brother.

In 2009, David was honored by Children's Health Magazine as one of the 25 most influential people in our children's lives over the last fifty years. Dave passed away in December, 2014, after a lengthy battle with cancer, following months of legislative research, bill writing and testimony for joint custody in behalf of children and parents in the State of Maryland. The Maryland State legislature continues to argue joint custody statues as of this writing.

Dr. Richard Sauber, a pioneer in the diagnosis and treatment of Parental Alienation provided me further appreciation for the human condition, and its reactions to change. A most reserved, bright, and humorous clinician, an outstanding and prolific author and forensic psychologist, it was Dr. Sauber who had especially encouraged me in my doctoral work since our first meetings at Children's Rights Council conferences in the 1990's, many which I had the privilege to coordinate. It was Dr. Sauber who very generously gave me his mother's painting, The Family, which soon served as the logo for the Toby Center for Family Transitions.

There are many casualties of divorce, but none more vulnerable than the children. So advocated Dr. Douglas Darnall, parenting researcher, alienation intervention practitioner, and educator. Dr. Darnall had written extensively, having devoted his professional life to training therapists and treating parents and their children who became emotionally immune, hateful or otherwise estranged from one or the other parent upon their separation and divorce. Though seriously ill, Dr. Darnall had so very kindly reviewed this manuscript prior to his passing in the summer of 2017. I had not known he was ill, he hadn't confided to me that he was. I shall remain always humbled by his confidence in this project and his quiet courage in support of this work. I met him numerous times over the years at conferences, and found Dr. Darnall assuring that the research content herein is vital for informing, educating, and supporting child outcomes.

There are a great many whom I want to thank since this handbook reflects the social research, personal journey, and guidance from many in academic programs and professional disciplines. I wish to first thank those who helped direct me to the sources of research and methodology.

With the guidance of my Advisor at The Union Institute & University, Dr. George Olshin, I studied the growing body of research on family, divorce, child custody and high conflict.

Attorney Steven Rauscher, Ph.D. served an intimate, daily guide in understanding findings. Friends for years, Steve and I shared an office suite while I managed my insurance practice, directed the Children's Rights Council of Connecticut and pursued arduously my doctorate. I recall asking Steve, a Professor and Chairman of the Department of Communications at the University of New Haven how to effectively manage my time. He replied, "run to the nearest fire." That has been my credo since.

Dr. Susan Horowitz, while clinical professor in the School of Medicine at the University of Rochester introduced me to the groundbreaking work of Dr. Urie Bronfenbrenner and his fundamental human ecology theory which he used to create the federally funded Healthy Start Program. Susie helped me to appreciate Bronfenbrenner's holistic theoretical approach to understanding family, the concept well embraced by university departments of Family Studies and organizations providing wraparound service programs. His theories inspired me to create The Toby Center for Family Transitions to serve families in crisis. Sadly, Susie passed away unexpectedly in 2010. Her love and friendship are missed by many.

I give my heartfelt thank you and love to Jean and Julius (Julie) Castagno, pioneers who fought for grandparents' rights to child access all the way to the Federal Supreme Court, and who welcomed my advocacy as a parent for similar rights. A writer and former teacher, Jean helped me with the writing of my doctoral research. Quite ironically, I had learned from Julius he was in my mother's high school class at Hartford High, and had a crush on her before joining the U.S. Army where he served with distinction during the Korean Conflict. I was visiting Jean and Julius in 2006 when Julius, a former medic, (finally) received highest praise from the Korean Government for Valor in saving lives of South Koreans pinned down by North Korean machine gunners while running through a minefield.

I offer special regards to Toby Center community partners in the faith based community including Father Joel Turmo, Father Mark Andrew, Father Andrew Sherman, Pastor Rob Maulella and their staff who pioneered support of holistic treatment through their gracious provision of their church facilities for therapeutic and supervised visitation and reunification programs.

I must mention, too, my special thanks to Rabbi Barry Silver, civil rights attorney, environmentalist, and former Florida State legislator. Rabbi Barry has served as a special advisor to me, has been a compassionate spokesman for co-parenting, and allowed me to share my voice on this topic. He has provided a unique role in addressing the confluence of the legal and faith based communities and very encouraging in this project.

There have been family judges, court administrators, therapists and policy makers who have inspired me through their own work to support joint custody, and heal families in transition. Many have disclosed frustrations with current systems, lack of funding for needed services, and need to clarify statutes to improve child access and decision making. I am grateful to their candid comments and trust.

Lastly, it is with great fondness and appreciation that I must thank Fabianna Dardati, Mary Ogden Ellis, wife of my mentor in supervised visitation, Alfred Ellis, and of course, Ellen Levy, wife of David Levy, the most significant and inspiring child advocate I've known, and my closest friend and mentor. Each of these individuals had taken this project from me to better format footnotes and review content so that I would indeed be able to complete this for publication to 'preserve family ties'.

Mark David Roseman, Ph.D.,
September 2017

INTRODUCTION

PURPOSE

As with any traumatic event, I believe there are three fundamental stages or attributes for recovery. To most effectively endure separation and marital breakup, I have found these *three attributes* for surviving, recovering, and moving forward:

Acknowledgement
Recognition
Support

Anyone who has successfully survived a most stressful event, indeed, a traumatic event, has done so through the acceptance, and application of these three vital principles; acknowledgment, recognition and support. All situations no matter the horror, the threats, the madness and the disappointments will cause responses that at some moment will bring these principles together.

I believe these three integrated concepts are truly the key constructs or fundamental approaches which we can give therapeutically and practically to ourselves and others to overcome any social, political, emotional and intellectual barrier. So many of these barriers are traumatic to us. Whether one survives sexual abuse, combat, or court, all must face at some moment, at some time, these and other distressing, and horrifying experiences will haunt and frighten us, and greatly reduce our ability to function. These experiences will inhibit our interpersonal relationships.

It is our interpersonal relationships that effect our perception of ourselves, of others, our community, and the world in which we live.

Our ability to cope is, I believe, the truth which we seek in order to sustain ourselves emotionally. It is that such life changing times for us require the availability of resources to help us 'best' cope, to deal with these frequently felt cataclysmic periods.

Our personal relationships, our love relationships, our interpersonal relationships with those we care about are among the most fragile of our relationships. We do not easily walk away from these relationships. Society does not accept our abandoning children, does not accept domestic violence perpetrated between and among household members. Academic, political and social pundits regularly debate the rate of divorce, its causes. The Federal Office of Child Support Enforcement sees the effects of single parenting through its frequently litigated child support revenue collections and Federal Department of Health and Human Services huge dollar authorization of TANF family support expenditures.

Society has enacted laws governing marital relationships and dissolution, and child access and visitation. Once one seeks change for these dynamics, then one invites a multitude of third parties to influence and determine our interrelationships going forward. These laws and the court process will affect the current generation with immediacy. These factors will affect parents and children for generations.

Among the most tragic, haunting and very common phenomenon to effect the way we relate with others, perceive our world, and which either strengthen our personal values, or create conflict within ourselves and our interpersonal relationships are those relationships in our household.

Look at the rates of child molestation, elder abuse, domestic violence, and divorce. They have skyrocketed in the last thirty years. Not only because of their voluntary reporting, police intervention and public court cases. We need to ask the causes. If we don't identify cause, if we don't understand, if we overlook and simply accept, then as a society, we are sunk.

The campaign for President of the United States in 2016 has brought so many issues to the forefront of TV, radio, internet. Race relations, immigration, gun control, international relations, economic policy, all have been so much more divisive because of their acknowledgement and presence in our society, our neighborhoods, and our homes. It is their presence that has brought acknowledgement, protest, research, and promises for change. Remedies for these divisive and significant social problems can only be successful when there is a national focus, regional support, and input from many walks of life to reflect on their experience, expectations, and beliefs.

Divorce has become a catalyst for murder, mayhem, and madness. It haunts over a million and a half parents and children annually. It inhibits their beliefs, effects their expectations. It is compounded by mysteries and expenses of legal procedure.

Bear with me please. For I believe, too, that anything, anything that we have experienced physically, or observed, even reacted to is based on our personal understanding of the world to that point. It is based on our reactions which are emotional, and which are generally unpredictable.

We know, too, that each of us, each one of us are, well, unique. We are different because our backgrounds and experiences are different. Our genders and gender expectations are different. Our ages are different. Our family histories are different, and especially because the family history for mom is different from the family history from dad.

There are many differences which affect our worldview. Therefore, it is also important that we step away from our divorce, at least for a minute, so we may see each moment, each day, and each procedure as a point of *context*.

Context is the most critical and relevant concept for our existence. It is not the purpose of our existence. Rather, context provides us the understanding of where we are now, in the moment, the result of what was.

Context is the precursor of what will be, in the short and likely the long term. Context is the perspective we each have of any activity, thought, and experience. It is shaped by our age at that moment, it is shaped by our ability to analyze and most clearly understand what this moment has been, who has shared that moment, and why that moment has occurred. We need to leave blame out of this while we develop our perspective. It is only then that we can achieve an emotional and physical and intellectual, and yes, a spiritual roadmap for enduring the frequently painful process of change, and improvement.

Let's please understand, that because of the differences, and if we allow others to be drawn into our situation, then we may also be effected by third party perspectives, and third party opinions, and third party prejudices. We must discern from whom we will get our support, and from whom we will obtain the help we need to move forward.

As divorce has become epidemic, so common, since the 1970's, there has been much written about it. How to survive divorce, how to cope as a single parent, how to fight in court, how to be a single parent, how to create new traditions for children, how to date and find a new sexuality, how to find the real love of our life, how to … how to make chicken soup! Well, this book is not written with so much opinion, so much biographic self-discovery, and so much personal advice.

This book is written as tool for you. It is written as a tool to help you understand the mess you're in, help you make sense of the journey you have undertaken, often alone. It is designed for attorneys, for therapists, for doctors, for educators, for judges, policy makers. It is written with years of research, love lost, and hope. It is written for you who wish to see child outcomes improved when parents separate.

Use the research in your litigation; use it to further your understanding of contemporary family dynamics. Use it to further explore new possibilities for trying divorce issues, for improving mediation techniques, for adopting new beliefs about marriage, love and yes, divorce.

This book was written for parents and family professionals so they might gain a fuller understanding of the causes and effects of parent separation, and the outcomes for parents and children that result when parents separate and divorce. We'll also explore single parenting, and the nature of household change when one parent, historically and most often the dad, leaves the original or 'nuclear' household and becomes the *absent* parent.

It's important for us to understand this for it is the family court system and family law statutes which provide labels for parents once they begin their legal process for child custody. One parent is rationalized as the 'away' parent, the 'non residential' parent, the 'non custodial' parent. The other parent with whom the child lives is coined also differently by other states as the 'at home' parent, the 'residential' parent, the 'custodial' parent.

This labeling can be demoralizing for one parent, and perhaps empowering for the other. Yet, this is the reality when the journey begins. A reality that affects all parties, each of the parents, the children, and the extended family – those formerly considered parents in law, brothers and sisters in laws, aunts, uncles, cousins. Mutual friends now also are perplexed, shocked, and frequently ostracized if they do not choose loyalty for one or the other parent.

Though it is said the divorce rate has appeared to stabilize nationally, it hovers at fifty percent of the marriage rate. Over 100,000 children annually will leave their world of two parent households where they will have played ball with dad, cooked with mom, vacationed with both, visited grandparents and cousins, gone to church or synagogue together, as a family. Suddenly, they will be thrust into a new home environment with one parent resident, or perhaps they'll have to move in with grandparents, maybe a parent's boyfriend or girlfriend's home, maybe taken to a shelter where privacy is no longer a reality either.

When parents separate, the children will enter a new reality, a more current Disney world with all too consuming fears of the unknown, unknown safety, unknown loyalty. Over 200,000 parents will enter their changed world of new responsibilities, changed perhaps conflicting priorities, suspicion, self doubt, fear, anger and hatred. Single and shared parenting, child custody, visitation, forensic evaluations, parental alienation will likely become new vocabulary and haunting experiences.

This book will provide an interdisciplinary and historical understanding of the sociological consequences when parents separate and divorce. I feel it vital for us to examine the interrelationships of human-behavior outcomes and the various roles that society play when parents separate and divorce. This understanding is vital if we are to also find new ways of approaching family transitions and the litigation process so that we may reduce negative outcomes for all family members when parents choose to separate.

To help you or your client cope with parental separation, I want you to understand the increasing and significant research on divorce and the issues—psychological, social, and financial—that families face before, during, and after parents separate. It is necessary to also consider the consequences of litigation, as well its emotional and behavioral impacts on parents and their children.

When parents decide to separate, many changes occur. Among the most notable are changed households and frequent court hearings to resolve matters of child custody, access (visitation), and child support.

Three questions should be asked:

1. How do these changes manifest themselves?
2. To what degree do they affect the children?
3. What might be done to mitigate negative consequences of parental separation and divorce?

When parents separate, seek child custody arrangements, or divorce, they go to court and face judges now charged with making decisions about child residency and child support, and appointing primary and non-custodial parents. How parents and children cope with these and other changes is a major focus of this book. Furthermore, how children and parents can and will transition positively with adaptive lifestyle change is the more important focus.

Yes, I have written this book to clearly show that children will have the best chance to thrive when both parents remain involved in their child's life. Children will fare best emotionally, when parents show attention, give unconditional love, and when parents demonstrate respect for each other in front of the children. This is not to say that single parents cannot succeed with parenting responsibilities. I do mean to reflect the conclusions shown by research that children have *the best* opportunity to adjust to a new lifestyle following their parents' breakup, when both parents remain responsibly engaged in their children's lives. That is not a difficult task, unless one or the other parent effectively 'blocks' the other from their children. It becomes most difficult for all when one parent will talk badly about the other to the children, thus denying them the love the absent parent has for them.

As a professor of Family Studies, I had routinely asked students to think of the time they may have had a relationship gone sour. "What was it like for you?" I would ask. Then, I would ask them to "not mover/' an inch, a muscle. "Remain still," I told them. "Now, look at your hands." Many were clenched. "What did you want to do following the breakup?" "Keep the ring"; "break his neck"; "scratch his car!"

"Why?" I asked.

"I wanted to punish, to get even," was often the reply.

I asked them to think what they might then do if they had had children in common. It was easy to see anger among some who remembered … It was easy to see punishment. "What is a parent's most prized 'possession'?" They'd answer, "our children." Couldn't punishment be all the more effective when these 'possessions' were used as the most punishing of tools? It wasn't too difficult for students to imagine that. For better than a third of students are now from single parent households.

Is the Court a place for punishment when parents choose to separate?

As a family mediator, I can answer this immediately.

No. Judges who have no training in child development, nor psychology, nor with an understanding of the grief process, or special needs parenting, of family research, none of this, will determine the parents legal involvement in the short term and the child's emotional (and behavioral) outcomes in the long term.

Judges have time only for facts, and their subliminal and biased views from their own family experience, and their own personal feelings.

Judges who lack such qualifications above govern family courts. So it was that the question of court intrusion in family lives following parental separation and divorce had guided me to my research and work since 1998.

I've been able to examine the world of sociological change that surrounds parental divorce, beginning just with that question. Consider: Child custody and child access are the primary parenting issues that are dissected, evaluated, and regulated by family courts.

Now, we can appreciate that family courts are cautious when making decisions about these matters, while parents remain circumspect about the complicated and intrusive court process. These parenting issues overwhelm the family courts with hearings that often last weeks, if not months. (Perhaps years if there's enough money for litigation.) Dissatisfied parents return to court frequently to demand compliance with orders or to modify prior judgments. Such proceedings affect tens of thousands of individuals year after year. It is common knowledge that with 100,000 divorces a year, there are 200,000 adults and nearly twice that number of children impacted. Consider, too, the many more thousands of grandparents, aunts, uncles, cousins, all extended family who also suffer from a household change.

I found research that suggests that child and parent outcomes are overwhelmingly negative for one third of families, at least for the short term (five years) when parents choose to separate and divorce. Rather than treating symptoms, perhaps professionals from different disciplines should look to all the difficult personal, social, community, and family dynamics and form partnerships to help mitigate those effects.

In what I'll call the 'Village' section, we'll examine a new vision for family intervention and new models for change. You will see several models for integrating numerous services for family members through interdisciplinary collaborations and protocols for protocols for professionals working with family members, particularly with assistance and treatment for children and parents suffering from highly conflicted separations.

As you'll find in this book, there are many opportunities for new standards, whether for intervention or for legal due process. *Preserving Family Ties* will guide you with new standards that may improve the process for families. If you wish for social change, then become a part by learning about these new potential standards, join with advocacy groups, nominate and vote for judges you believe will lead the way in reforming family law process in your jurisdiction.

I want for you to know that you are not alone. At least know that there are others who are and have experienced many of the exact same pressures you or your client do. We'll look at parent separation in the context of cultural changes that have occurred over the last fifty years, and then consider the current realities of parent separation. Because many communities today are found to be culturally diverse, it is necessary for us to consider the relationship between family dynamics and culture. Power and expectation do not cross cultural divides equally; nor does family law take into account cross-cultural interpretations. Therefore, discussion of cultural misunderstandings and appropriate community resources will be emphasized.

Having known cases where brides have been imported and where culturally and ethnically distinct individuals have married, I believe it is also important to at least have a general recognition of the challenges they each bring into their union, and marriage dissolution.

Preserving Family Ties examines procedures, decision-making, and reasons for existing judicial process. It adds import to new learning that identifies effects of parent separation on themselves, their children, and society.

We will first address the evolution of contemporary family dismantling processes and beliefs from the perspective of children and their parents who are separated or divorced. Included are extensive references to research and interviews with professionals from law, medicine, education, and psychology.

Preserving Family Ties has been guided by criticisms of current custody law, the divorce process, and the grave, sensitive and oft sensational side effects produced by the current legal procedures. These criticisms have been raised by numerous parents, psychotherapists, social service agency caseworkers, health providers, and attorneys that I have interviewed since the beginning of my own divorce actions in 1997. I have categorized these complaints and reframed them below as questions:

1. Despite their overburdened caseload, should a family court judge or magistrate take the time in individual hearings to address the fear and confusion that parents endure when litigating separation agreements, custody, and child access orders?
2. Might it be helpful for the presiding justice to assume that these emotional conditions are present in most of their cases?
3. Should these judges acknowledge that children will mirror, or respond in some way, to their parents' angst at home?
4. For how long might judges preside over the same case in districts where it is normal for judges to be transferred through periodic rotation to different courts every two years?

It may be helpful to incorporate these questions in a district court or regional survey to gather information for use in improving court protocols. Each practitioner surveyed might find that the questions themselves result in an elevated awareness of parent/child/client outcomes related to existing legal procedures. While the social or health services family professional and legal practitioner to ponder these questions, they may also consider the mental and physical effects accompanying custody and child access litigation.

Support systems for these families are few; much of society's policy remains centered on the traditional nuclear family which has characterized the American household for generations. Rather, family deficiencies and weaknesses are addressed through specific agency programs such as parent education and psychological or therapeutic services. Members of nontraditional families are generally ignored by educators, are poorly supported by the religious communities, and are seldom identified by other professionals who work with these family members. Other professions, such as medicine and law, even educators, generally stay focused on their respective services and neither consider nor inquire further into their client's attitudes, emotional states or family dynamics. Clergy arguable who have great and regular opportunity to assist their communities seldom venture into congregants' lives when these lives are impacted by challenge and instability. Yet, as being among the first to see these changes, they remain silent and lose the chance to prevent or contain, to intervene when conflict and abhorrent behaviors arise, when children exhibit sadness and lethargy.

Therefore, family professionals will benefit particularly from a common understanding of the complexities found in child and family outcomes when parents separate. I will draw upon reports, statistics, and research from numerous fields, including psychology, law, policy, education, sociology, and medicine. This information provides the backdrop for considering cause, effect, and relationships among the myriad factors that influence family dynamics, family structure, and individual outcomes.

I think you'll find this information identifies and explains the trends in parent separations, divorce, custody awards, and shared parenting (visitation) and then well relates behavioral factors to individual, child, and family outcomes. We all need to have this shared understanding. Those now separated will struggle through it because of their many emotional feelings. For you, I ask you to please take the time to read this book at least twice. Then, share it with your attorney, your therapist, your client, and your former partner.

Why?

When we can all share this understanding, when everyone is "on the same page," then the synchronicity for healing will be far more powerful, far more effective. There will be new professional collaborations possible and that may help identify dysfunction and its sources and make family structural changes less disturbing by treating these dysfunctions. Treatment then will be more effective when family professionals can partner through holistic treatment plans, incorporating psychotherapy, medical help, education, and spiritual renewal.

Successful adaptation to a changed family dynamic can best be accomplished when professionals from different disciplines are willing to seek a better understanding of their interrelated purposes. I propose new interventions—including interdisciplinary collaborations among professionals—to improve social, emotional, physical, and achievement outcomes.

My hope is that, based on their common understanding, these professionals will work together to bring about positive and more predictable outcomes for family members.

My hope for the parent is that once they can accept their new reality, once they can recognize that they are not alone, they will then find the support mechanisms to help them provide the emotional and financial foundations to go forward with a new, exciting and meaningful life. As a divorced parent, I do understand much about divorce and parenting so much better.

As a consequence, and based on my doctoral work spanning ten years, I've found research findings which so clearly demonstrate that coping mechanisms for parental separation and divorce will be best attained with multiple interventions from law, psychology and therapy, education, medicine and self care, all interrelated. It is further found that by offering such "interdisciplinary practical and healing modalities" (Janet Roseman, Ph.D., Nova University School of Medicine) then children and parents will best thrive.

In 2008, I designed a unique solution, a holistic model for encouraging, not treating, parents who are living the hells of unrequited separation, of punitive behaviors from a former lover, of the loss of family ties when parents choose to separate. This became the basis for my founding the Toby Center for Family Transitions (www.thetobycenter.org) as a single and familiar location for most resources necessary for family change, and healing.

It is my hope that those professionals working with families will better understand the challenges that parents and children cannot easily avoid. Furthermore, it is my expectation that those professionals who possess the compassion for their clients, commitment towards helping them better adjust to life change due to separation, divorce and child custody orders will apply new understandings in their work.

I cannot help but believe that we all must work to improving child outcomes. Whether it takes a village to raise a child or not, research shows that social values demand we all work together politically, legislatively, practically, compassionately to assure children that they have the fortune to choose their lifestyle from a point of emotional stability, good physical health, and appropriate boundaries for respect and tolerance upon which our very own societal freedoms are based.

I appreciate you on taking this important time to read, to study the research, to apply the concepts and truths about child custody. In *Preserving Family Ties*, you have a valuable tool to help your client, to help your child. Your new knowledge will help you grow personally, professionally, and therefore, to improve the social fabric of your community, and our society at large.

PART I

THE SOCIAL CONFLICTS
OF THE FAMILY

CHAPTER 1

THE STATE OF THE FAMILY: DIVORCE, CUSTODY, AND CHILDREN

THE DEMOGRAPHICS OF THE FAMILY

The divorce rate in the United States has seen great change over the last thirty years. According to the National Center for Health Statistics, "43 percent of first marriages end in separation or divorce within 15 years."[1] These 1996 figures represent a four-fold increase since 1970, according to the US Department of Commerce.[2]

Using data from the US Bureau of the Census, Grall found that from 1980 to 1997 the number of children living in two-parent households dropped "among all racial and ethnic groups."[3] The Census Bureau estimated that

1. nearly one-third of all children under age twenty-one live in one-parent households;
2. 85 percent live with custodial mothers; and
3. 15 percent live with custodial fathers.

According to the US Bureau of the Census, there are some telling statistics on household structures.[4] Trends for the new millennium show that fewer children are residing in dual-parent households; some 68 percent of children live in two-parent households compared to 77 percent in 1980.[5] The numbers of children living with two parents are greatest for white parents, followed by Hispanic parents (64 percent). Just 35 percent of African American children live in two-parent households.[6]

Mother-only households number 24 percent, while 6 percent live with their father and another 4 percent live without a parent.[7] The census found that many children live with grandparents or have some form of family foster care. Grandparent households are growing rapidly, having doubled from 3 percent of all children under age eighteen to 6 percent in 1996. This statistic is especially noteworthy when we account for racial differences. "Thirteen percent of black children reside with their grandparents compared to 4 percent for whites and 7 percent for Hispanics."[8] This is particularly so for inner-city children whose parents are absent, incarcerated, or in various confining rehabilitation programs. Teen pregnancy, which is highest among African Americans, helps to inflate these numbers.

Children who live in a household with one parent are considerably more likely to have family incomes below the poverty line than are children who grow up a household with two parents. "Nearly 48 percent of metro children in mother-only families were poor in 2000, in contrast to 10 percent of non-metro children."[9]

Poverty rates are also associated with education levels. According to the same USDA data, children living with parents who have less than a high school education are three times more likely to live at the poverty level and six times more likely to be impoverished than those with at least one year of college.

"The payment of child support could also have indirect effects by enhancing the well-being of the mother by reducing her economic worries. It may also have non-economic effects such as improving the quality of the mother-father or father-child relationship by reducing conflict between the parents."[10]

The aim herein is to examine major effects of divorce upon children and parents. The nature and extent of these negative effects depend on many factors, which will be explored. It is important to acknowledge that parents can and do choose to separate and that such separation may not resolve their respective complaints (such as fear, loss of love, or boredom). Further, the separation may not improve the family's dynamic. Yet it is a parent's right to separate, whether in perfect agreement or with great disappointment, anger, and hostility.

Age may be a significant variable when considering parent separations. "Current projections now indicate that the proportion [of those divorcing] could be as high as 50 percent for persons now in their early forties,"[11] whereas the divorce rate hovers around one-third for men and women after age 60 in their first marriage.

Cohabiting parents are statistically more likely to separate than parents who are married. Compared with married couples, who have a 20 percent likelihood of divorce within the first five years, unmarried couples have a 49 percent chance of breaking up within five years. After ten years, unmarried couples are found to break up at a rate of 62 percent, nearly twice the 33 percent breakup rate of married couples.[12]

McLanahan and Garfinkle found that "when a child is born out-of-wedlock, at least half of those couples are actively contemplating marriage as an option for themselves. Yet the current system simply says we don't want to talk about that option for you; we simply want to make sure you establish paternity and get a child support order in place."[13]

A survey commissioned by the National Fatherhood Initiative found that those who married in their mid-20s were less likely to divorce than those who married before the age of twenty.[14] The survey found the divorce rate to be 50 percent for those marrying at this young age. Another study found that the rate of divorce was reduced by half—to 24 percent—when marriage was delayed till after age twenty-five.[15]

With respect to divorce and race, Cherlin found a disparity between African Americans and whites when comparing those born in the 1950s. He found that 50 percent more white women married than black women and that the rate of divorce among black couples greatly exceeded that of whites through 1995.[16] He found that Hispanic marriage and divorce rates were closer to those of whites. However, data show that separated Hispanic and black couples were less likely to complete the divorce process, which also correlates to family income.[17]

It may be that resistance to divorce is a cultural phenomenon, not at all related to income. Though marriage failures and parental separations cross socioeconomic categories, further relationships need to be examined with respect to home life, educational levels, child-rearing experiences, and personal expectations.

Smith writes, "One of the primary reasons that the divorce rate is so high among black families (60 percent, compared to 50 percent in whites) is because there is a lack of true communication between black males and their mates. This can be attributed in part to a black man's self-image. Many black men grow up in an environment of constant conflict or indifference, and self-protection becomes more important than self-love and emotional growth."[18]

It may be helpful to note measures of reconciliation following separation and divorce among previously married couples. "Approximately 10 percent of all currently married couples (9 percent of white women and 14 percent of black women) in the U.S. have separated and divorced."[19] Why might the rate of reconciliation be higher for black Americans than that for whites? Possibly because of "marriage squeeze," a low number of men identified as eligible bachelors due to unemployment, mortality, and imprisonment.[20]

Divorce and public policy appear to be intertwined when we review divorce statistics on a regional basis. If we examine the geopolitical landscape, we may find some interesting statistics. Consider that the neoconservative "red states" have been found to have divorce rates that are 25 percent higher than those of liberal "blue states."[21] "All the major broadcast networks and all the cable news outlets utilized the same color scheme: red for Republicans and blue for Democrats."[22] These labels do not accurately represent voters since the electoral process requires each state to dedicate all its votes to the winning candidate. Therefore, it is conceivable that more examination of religious values, marriage ages, patriarchal values, alcoholism, and family violence may be helpful in an initial review to determine reasons for differentiation. Thorough statistical research on these factors and domestic violence outcomes may offer explanations of divorce rate differences between red and blue states. Such research might identify predictable variations and suggest appropriate geographic and cultural opportunities for intervention.

If marital or cohabitation conditions can be used to predict such family dismantling, then there could be societal interventions to reduce their number. The state of Florida advocates premarital counseling and offers couple discounts for the marriage license fee if they undertake a course outlined in Florida's Marriage Preparation and Preservation Act, passed in 1998.[23]

There is a range of causes for parent separation. For example, experts have found that men and women differ emotionally, and these emotional differences may help account for marital breakdowns. Men are unable to admit their emotional losses and frequently internalize their feelings. Levant believes that men have been socialized and preconditioned to limit "their vulnerable feelings including fear, hurt and shame."[24] Furthermore, Levant found that men have "difficulty with emotional intimacy," and "difficulties in becoming full partners with their wives in maintaining a home and raising children."[25]

If such issues are not addressed professionally, it is more likely that parents will opt to self-medicate with drugs, tobacco, and alcohol. Indeed, domestic violence and suicide might also result, injuring and victimizing parents, children, and others.

The ultimate traumatic event that parents may face is the loss of their children. This loss is either physical, emotional, or both. The loss that parents feel when they separate is reflected in the following discussion of custody and child access (visitation).

CHILD CUSTODY AND CHILD ACCESS (VISITATION)

The urgency of working with family professionals cannot be overstated since each year the parents of more than one million children choose to separate. That the experience is traumatic for children and for their parents cannot be minimized.

"Divorce is a time of tremendous upheaval in families. Given this disruption, should the divorce process occur at a point where the child's attachment style is not fully developed, it stands to reason that the likelihood of secure attachment developing is reduced."[26]

Custody follows as the most contested issue litigated in family courts. Current practice is based on nineteenth-century court decisions where custody of the children, because of their economic value, was awarded to the father. Today, custody proceedings are lengthy and emotional, with legal jousting to determine with which parent the child will live. Accompanying this decision is the determination of when, where, and why the noncustodial parent will have access to the child. When, during the marriage, such issues as recreation and bedtime would normally have been resolved between the parents themselves, now a third-party court system enters the fray. "Most states simply offer a gender-neutral law requiring judges to apply an elusive "best interests of the child" standard or they mandate a preference for joint custody, asking judges to divide the child's life."[27]

The greatest conceptual change for families has been that of joint custody. Joint custody is the legal status that two parents enjoy when the law acknowledges their continuing involvement with—parenting of—their children. This status is defined by the laws of the state where the people reside. "On divorce of the child's parents, the court has power to award custody of the child to one parent, with or without visitation rights to the other, or jointly to both parents. During the pendency of divorce proceedings [period between initial court filings and final court orders] the court may order temporary custody of children. Legal custody encompasses the right to make all decisions concerning the child's welfare, education, religion, growth, and development."[28] Residential custody is the second, most contested, of the two. The court first separates the two custody types and determines with which parent the child will live, either mom or dad. The court will then specify the rights of each parent to participate in continuing decision making affecting the child's schooling, religious observances, medical care, and recreation.

Joint custody is the cause for most recurring legal arguments. As Levy states below, there are fifty thousand recurring custody cases each year, added to the thousands of new cases being litigated. Associated costs are high and the emotional effects are greatest when parents battle for custody and child access. It may be that possession of the child represents power to the custodial parent. When their child resides with them, the custodial parent may believe himself or herself validated as a competent parent as well as blameless for the marriage failure.

Regardless of whose home is assigned as the primary residence for the child, decisions about child rearing rest with the primary or custodial parent. It remains very difficult for a nonresident parent to influence the child on a daily basis. Friedman finds that "joint custody is at least as likely as alternative custody arrangements are to result in diffusion of responsibility for the child. When both take responsibility it is tantamount to neither doing so."[29] According to Ahrons and Wallisch, determining custody is "the most difficult and complex task of the divorce process."[30] Yet Braver points out that "if each parent is empowered by joint legal custody and is allowed involvement in the full variety of child rearing activities, few parents, or children will feel deprived."[31]

In my work with client families since 1998, I've found that those parents who cooperate, who diligently focus on the common goal for children to be happy, healthy and well cared for, will find that children will well adjust to separated parents. Parents who acknowledge their roles to share in parenting responsibilities will communicate regularly with each other, and harbor no resentment towards time each spends with their children.

Sadly, among the thirty percent of parents who divorce with anger and resentment, there will be many who will sabotage each other, cancel scheduled visitation time, and not comply with court ordered supervised visitation. They will not agree to schedule changes, they will accuse each other of abusing the children, they will call DCF on each other. Indeed, they will not share each other's needs, nor accommodate to each other's needs. The children, therefore, are not the priority as found in the bio nuclear family; they are last.

Results of court ordered custody arrangements have lifelong effects on children, parents, and extended family members. Braver writes, "The findings for joint legal custody samples indicate that children do not actually show better adjustment, but it is important to note that joint legal custody children typically spend a substantial amount of time with the father as well."[32]

Bauserman's recent meta-analysis of child custody outcomes provides an important backdrop for new court decisions and public policies aimed at children from dismantled homes. Bauserman found that children in shared custody situations were no worse off than those in nuclear or intact households. He investigated thirty-three research studies that examined 1,846 children in sole custody and 814 children in joint custody. He then chose a sample of some two hundred children from intact families and compared the data with that of all groups.[33]

Bauserman examined their emotional health and found no difference in rates of low self-esteem and behavior between these two populations. However, he found that many children of sole custody and single-parent households were markedly worse off. "It was the sole-custody parents who reported higher levels of current conflict," whereas his research demonstrated that "joint custody actually reduces parental conflict over time."[34] Bauserman notes that joint custody was not the panacea; but what mattered was that the two parents were actively engaged in child rearing.

CHILD CUSTODY AND LITIGATION

Child custody and child access are matters that occupy more court time than other divorce-related hearings because of their importance to parents. "In divorce proceedings, the most difficult aspect for children (as well as parents) to overcome is the issue of which parent is going to maintain custody."[35] These issues are both personal and paramount for parents, as reflected in Dunn's findings that "the impact of custody arrangements on the quality of children's relationships with all their parents deserves attention."[36]

Both custody and child access are usually argued in court simultaneously since seeing one's children and nurturing one's children are primary concerns for legally recognized parents who may be single, separated, divorced, or never married. These matters become most difficult when paternity cannot be proven on a child's birth certificate.

Some family attorneys, psychotherapists, judges, and the research affirm that the legal process is damaging to family members. It continues to foment hostility between two parties seeking the prize of primary custody of their child and therefore control over the child's access to the departed or absent parent. Significantly, it is at the beginning of the parental breakup or disentanglement that the attitudinal tone and goals for subsequent custodial and visitation litigation is most profound. Parents' feelings of fear, animosity, and anger are most pronounced at this time. Litigation (with attorney representation) often plays off these feelings, positioning for power and control.

Illinois attorney Jeffrey Leving wrote, "Frankly, domestic relations proceedings often resemble a midnight walk through unfamiliar countryside. The legal terrain a man must traverse to remain his children's father is tangled with thick underbrush and dangerous canyons, but it's not always a landscape composed entirely of rocks and hard places."[37]

In the litigation or adversarial process, there will be parents who feel some measure of victory while others will feel some measure of loss. These feelings result from their subjective satisfactions in the litigation process. Karin Huffer writes, "The fact is that whenever events are so profoundly dramatic, shocking, disturbing, or long lasting, they exponentially jeopardize one's ability to function effectively."[38] According to Braver, "Women feel more satisfied with their divorce settlements for two reasons: because they are more likely to get the deal they want than men are, and because they feel they have greater influence over the settlement process than men do." [39] Braver concludes that women feel the most empowered in the divorce process. Dr. Joyce Arditti found that men felt treated "unfairly" by the family court process. Family courts have the opportunity to improve the lot of those parents and children who feel the need of support from a responsible and caring society.

It had not been enough, however, that the research showed the disparities in the treatment of men in the courts as custodial parents or parents who should have more than 'cookie cutter' time sharing with their children. Similarly, it had not been appropriate for courts not to enforce court orders for child support when such payments were infrequent, ignored, or examined separately from child access (visitation) scheduling.

Joint custody statutes needed to be written, placed, and complied with.

In 1986 Leving helped craft a model state statute, a legal mechanism to serve as the means to reduce tactical abuse allegations. This statute was Illinois's joint custody legislation known as the Illinois Marriage and Dissolution of Marriage Act. Its approach was to limit the emotional damage from custody challenges. The key concept became the Illinois child custody statute, ss.750 ILCS (5) (602.1), as follows: "The court shall presume that the maximum involvement and cooperation of both parents regarding the physical, mental, moral, and emotional well-being of their child is in the best interests of the child."[40]

The Illinois law is similar to that of many of the forty-four states that permit joint custody; it excludes the presumption that both parents have legal and enforceable parenting rights. According to the statute, "There shall be no presumption in favor of or against joint custody but upon the application of either or both parents, or upon its own motion, the court shall consider an award of joint custody."[41] Continuing, the statute states, "The court may enter an order of joint custody if it determines that joint custody would be in the best interests of the child, taking into account the following:

1. The ability of the parents to cooperate effectively and consistently in matters that directly affect the joint parenting of the child. *Ability of the parents to cooperate* means the parents' capacity to substantially comply with a Joint Parenting Order. The court shall not consider the inability of the parents to cooperate effectively and consistently in matters that do not directly affect the joint parenting of the child;
2. The residential circumstances of each parent; and
3. All other factors that may be relevant to the best interests of the child.[42]

According to recent data from the American Bar Association, just twenty-one of these states have statutes that automatically presume that joint custody may be awarded. Eight states support joint custody if the parents can agree to it or demonstrate in court why it should be awarded to both. Twelve states require the parent objecting to joint custody to provide evidence why "the opposing" parent should be denied any custody rights. Six states, including Alabama, Arkansas, Georgia, West Virginia, and North and South Dakota, have had no joint custody protections till recently either de facto or by statute. New York ratified joint custody in 2010. Florida now mandates fifty-fifty as a starting point for joint custody (shared parenting) for mothers and fathers. Maryland and Massachusetts do not yet have joint custody legislation. Connecticut custody statute now requires joint custody, unless one objects, thereby placing the burden of proof on the other party who is the target for that objection.

"Despite its rapid acceptance by most American jurisdictions in one form or another, joint custody remains controversial among family law scholars, child welfare experts, and feminists," writes Herma Kay.[43] Yet increasingly, the notion that parents continue to share custody of their children is becoming reality. "Parents, judges, and child experts are becoming increasingly aware of the necessity of having both parents involved in children's lives; this can be made possible by joint or shared custody."[44]

David Levy has pointed out that "there are still 50,000 continuing child custody battles in this country every year (about 5 percent of all divorces) representing the highest conflict. That is a huge number of cases in the court system because they are devouring so much time and expense with court time including judges, sheriffs, forensic evaluators, family relations case managers, and more. How can anyone state absorb so many cases each year on a cumulative basis? Not to mention parallel litigation for child support modification that often accompanies highly contested child custody."[45]

Many parents fear that without an agreement between them, the courts expect litigation. Parents fear that judgments interpreted as being in the best interests of the children are being made by a court system that does not know their children, or them, well. Borrell-Carrio et al. observe that "judges have no special training to help them deal with families in crisis. They are charged with safeguarding the best interests of children without knowledge about the specific needs of children at different developmental stages."[46]

Without a written statute specifying the court's understanding of any issue at hand, there is no baseline or standard for a family court judge to compare or measure requirements for litigated outcomes. Unless clarified in court orders, joint custody is difficult to preserve, and there is no protection of parental interests to assure each continuing involvement in their children's lives short of court-ordered child support payments.

The complexity of child access has become difficult to monitor. The "he said, she said" argument about children's health and availability or desires for visitation, if pursued, ordinarily leads to forensic psychological evaluations and subpoenaing of doctors, educators, neighbors, and others. It delays access and can lead to the vilification of the litigating, noncustodial parent by the primary or custodial parent.

Child support is generally interpreted by the courts as solely financial. Therefore, it is measurable in dollars and compliance is easily monitored. Noncompliance with support orders may trigger imprisonment or the threat thereof, particularly if the noncustodial father is at fault. Unlike with monetary child support, interruption of child access seldom results in threatened or imposed punitive measures such as fines, house arrest, or prison.

Pearson acknowledges, "Like nonpayment of child support, non-visitation is a complex issue, with many causes. And like child support disputes, access problems are often rooted in problems that are not easily addressed in brief problem-solving interventions ... As is also true of child support enforcement, a variety of remedies are needed to help parents resolve their visitation disputes."[47]

There are many noncustodial dads who believe the court system is unfair, particularly when upholding their children's rights to visitation. Braver's research findings confirm reasons for this perception. "The fact that there aren't many effective sanctions available to the court when a mother has interfered with visitation (access) has unfortunately convinced fathers that there is a gender bias at work in the system upholding their concerns."[48]

As in some states (such as Florida and Wisconsin), it may be that mandated negotiation (mediation) between the parties and parenting agreements will lead to more equitable court orders in family courts. Several states do mandate such efforts at resolution, but court remains the only viable option when parents are otherwise uncompromising.

FINANCIAL EFFECTS AND THE WORKPLACE

Financial effects of divorce, custody, and child access issues are extraordinary if they are examined on both the macro (societal) and micro (familial) levels. "To the extent that poverty, poor health, juvenile delinquency and school problems are produced by divorce, then there are larger economic consequences than the approximate $11 billion annual costs including those on state and federal governments."[49]

The Federal Department of Health and Human Services stated in a 1996 memo that children of single-parent households suffer when a parent, statistically more often the father, is absent from the home. Relating these micro and macro effects in the context of expenses to society, it is more than notably impressive to see the impact that litigation and its social effects have in the country.

One's place of employment is, like the public school for children, a place where working adults spend most of their waking hours. An employee or business owner works to earn income to support a certain lifestyle, as well as family members including dependent children. Workers are thus motivated to go to work, undertake work responsibilities, and contribute to company productivity.

When an employee is emotionally burdened by anger and sadness from a failing relationship, his or her productivity may decrease. Divorce and child custody hearings and related court proceedings require the employee to leave work frequently and for many workday hours. An employee's emotional distractions, combined with physical absences from work, may seriously impede the employer's workflow. "While the human toll is obvious, there can also be a bottom-line impact from lost output, increased absenteeism and increased health care costs."[50] Andrews suggests that human resource managers identify their high-risk workers at company facilities and prepare for any family-related stresses that an employee might exhibit. She finds that the most vulnerable workers are those who:

- earn less than $25,000 annually,
- do not have a college degree,
- live in disadvantaged neighborhoods,
- have no religious affiliation, and
- live in the South, Midwest, or West.

A potentially serious problem for employers is that anxious employees may want to unburden themselves by confiding in other employees at inappropriate times. "Employees getting divorced face a seemingly endless stream of legal, financial, housing, and child care decisions."[51] They need immediate help and may be so overwhelmed that they turn to their colleagues to vent and find guidance. Says Nancy Terry, a clinical care manager in an Employee Assistance Program (EAP) in Research Triangle Park, N.C., "If they go to work and talk nonstop about their divorce, they may end up impacting both their productivity and the productivity of others."[52]

Many parents find themselves financially overburdened and feeling "abandoned" by the legal system in child access and custody proceedings meant to retain their parenting rights and their relationships with their children. These parents do not easily recover emotionally from the war to free their children from the other parent's control.

CHILD ACCESS AND PARENTAL CONFLICT

Courts must deal with a tangled web of emotional conflict, psychological motivations, and practical decision-making. Their job is doubly difficult when parental conflict accompanies divorce, custody, and child access determinations. Rulings for sole custody are most frequent, particularly when conflicts between parents appear to be irresolvable. When such conflict is present, Maccoby and Mnookin find joint custody "a more radical alternative to the present best interests custody standard".[53]

Braver found that 30 percent of fathers interviewed stated that they were denied visitation privileges "at least once."[54] Author Gail Sheehy declared that "the newer reality is the Deadbolted Dad— locked out of his children's hearts after divorce with little attention paid to enforcing or honoring their visitation rights."[55]

Braver's data also show that more than 35 percent of noncustodial fathers and fifteen percent of noncustodial mothers believe that custody and access litigation will prove discouraging and unsuccessful.

Corroborating this was the federal report by a quarter of mothers interviewed who admit to denial of visitation.[56] Nearly 40 percent of all noncustodial parents practically disappear from their children's lives because of diminished access to their children, increased emotional pain, and the artificial nature of an imposed child access/ visitation schedule.

Braver asserts that joint custody needs to be the goal for each litigating parent and that joint custody is both supported by and enforced by state statute. "Joint legal custody and very substantial contact with both parents ... should be the rebutting presumption, which could be challenged by either party in divorce cases. This would assure both parents in most families that they will retain their fundamental parental roles with the children."[57] Furthermore, Braver continues,

> If one parent wished to deprive the other of this minimal level of parental disenfranchisement, that parent should have the burden of proving his or her plan is more clearly in the child's best interests. We believe, if this standard were the guideline, it would substantially lower the stakes for deciding the next 30 percent of the child's time, that is, which parent was declared the child's residential parent. Parents fight, argue, and litigate when they feel they are being deprived of something, when they are being made to lose. With this minimum standard, few parents should feel they would suffer a loss. As a result, most couples should be able to come to an amicable physical custody and visitation agreement and define for themselves what's in their own particular child's best interests, perhaps with the help of mediation.[58]

This conclusion by Braver and O'Connell suggests that when state law protects the rights of each parent to continue parenting without (court) interference, then the parents will do just that. They will continue to parent their child. But joint custody does not suggest that physical custody need be shared on a fifty-fifty basis. Courts might review the parenting duties allotted during cohabitation and seek to protect parents' rights to continue carrying out these duties. Court decisions should also be revisited as the developmental needs of the children change as they mature.

The federal government provides protections for consumers, fair trade, and school achievement. However, it is important to clarify that there is no uniform or federal standard for states to rule in courts of family law. Rather, each state is autonomous in its regulations and therefore has its own set of statutes. State family law statutes, conference presentations, and many legislators all corroborate that it is the individual state that has jurisdiction over marriage and divorce. Gregory, Swisher, and Scheible-Wolf assert state that "the state's right to regulate such marital relations is *not absolute,* and is subject to constitutional limitations if the state regulation is arbitrary, unreasonable or capricious."[59] It is most difficult for anyone to argue before a federal court on constitutional grounds since it is the state's mandate in which the parties reside that governs the decisions of the respective family court.

Most family courts require divorcing parents to enroll in a state-mandated parenting class prior to the granting of final orders for custody and child access and divorce. "More than half of the family courts nationwide currently offer services for divorcing families, yet few of these programs have been tested to determine whether they foster positive gains."[60] There is little documentary evidence yet that correlates behavior and/or attitudinal changes with course satisfaction. "Separating and divorcing parents who attend parent education programs consistently report high levels of satisfaction. Although reassuring, these findings do not demonstrate that parent education programs actually change the way parents relate to one another and their children ... The programs were somewhat less successful in reducing conflicts over child custody, access, and litigation between parents."[61]

The litigation process is designed to produce a victor. By itself, it is not an arbitration process. So, as with other litigants, it effectively charges moms and dads to seek a winning position. Parents have been frustrated because litigation takes much time, having been advanced through separate legal motions.

Susan Horwitz, PhD, of the University of Rochester School of Medicine, said in a conversation, "Love belongs to couples; children belong to parents. Divorce is one set of issues; custody is another."[62] This process, referred to in legal parlance as bifurcation, seeks what the attorneys perceive as a practical approach to these family issues. It is normally how family courts proceed with marital separation and child issues including custody and visitation. The problems with litigation remain, however, because each matter brings its own applicable emotional charge to the court action while abruptly ripping away what may have been a well integrated foundation involving affection, control, and family.

The birth of a child often represents a couple's emotional commitment. Efforts by one or both parties to disentangle this love relationship can be most formidable and destructive. The emotional process is not well understood by the courts, few judges have any background in psychology, and heavy caseloads do permit little time to account for it.

However, if the emotional upheaval were to be acknowledged by the courts, then the courts might be better positioned to provide supportive interventions. The process might then lead to more appropriate decisions for children and their parents.

Consider that litigation is often characterized by expenditure of time and money (thousands of dollars). It may be that less acrimonious alternatives to protracted litigation may be less expensive and less emotionally destructive. Less time in court may be associated with far fewer legal expenses and therefore less cost, more opportunities for child access, and improved communication between parents. These results may certainly be better for the child and commitments towards such processes might be best for the parents and the best interests of the child. Let's discuss what the courts have identified as being in the children's best interests.

Best Interests of the Child Standard vs. Tender Years Doctrine

A primary consideration of family court judges is what is referred to in the legal canon of family law as the "children's best interests." According to the American Bar Association, "If the parents cannot agree on custody of their child, the courts decide custody based on *the best interests of the child*. Determining the child's best interests involves many factors, no one of which is the most important factor."[63]

"Best interests" are universally cited by judges at family court hearings as the "reason" for the judge's ruling. Where the child will live post-parent separation (residential custody) and when the absent or nonresidential parent may interact with the child are all decisions based on the children's best interests.

Judges are neither trained psychologists, nor are they trained in child development. Yet they frequently relate their custody and access orders to the children's best interests. They do so with assumed privilege stemming from the pivotal nineteenth-century New York custody case, *People v. Mercein*.[64] The case is mentioned now because of its influence on custody rulings since then. "The 'general doctrine' that a father had 'an absolute right to the custody of his child, if personally unobjectionable,' was not sustained by the law of this state. Instead, courts exercised 'sound discretion' in pursuit solely of the child's best interests."[65]

Initially, the child's-best-interests interpretation was used to support custody awards to fathers who needed their children for farm labor and for inheriting family property. The above case began with a writ of separation signed in 1838 by John and Eliza Barry providing the intentions to live separately. When Eliza moved into her father, Thomas Mercein's, home, John apparently coveted the children (and her).

This concept remains with today's family court judges who often justify their decisions by referring to the "children's best interests." Whereas custody awards to fathers have historically exceeded such awards to mothers, this favoritism began to change after the Civil War when many men were killed and when machinery began to improve the efficiency of agricultural production. More commonly, courts imputed a legal principle known as the "tender year's doctrine." "Other things being equal, if the child was of 'tender years' (generally pre-teenage), recent tradition all but automatically gave custody to the mother."[66] This rule was identified as most important for the children, particularly very young infants and toddlers. The tender years doctrine was deemed the most appropriate defense for awarding custody to the mother since it was determined that only the mother could best provide a child with the nurturing and care they required during their formative period. With the tender year's presumption, family courts found that the mother was the parent most able to care for the children. "Several states have struck down the doctrine as violative of equal protection or of a state ERA (Equal Rights Amendment). Others have upheld the doctrine against constitutional challenge."[67]

The tender year's doctrine lasted through the late 1960s when, in most states, it was replaced by the "gender-neutral best interests of the child doctrine, under which there is no presumption for either the mother or the father." The recent research conducted by Julie Artis suggests a different reality. She surveyed family court decisions across the country, examining whether custody decisions could be attributed to either the tender years doctrine or the gender-neutral "child's best interest." [68]

In her analysis, Artis found that judges who ruled with best-interests guideline awarded custody of young children to their mothers 84.2 percent of the time. Her research found that judges who ruled with respect to the tender years doctrine awarded custody to mothers in nearly all cases. Only in hotly contested custody cases did she find custody awards to be more equally distributed. She states that in her interviews with family court judges, "even judges who oppose the tender year's doctrine acknowledged that they might award custody to mothers a majority of the time."[69]

In a 1990 study, the National Center for Health Statistics found that fathers received sole custody only 8.5 percent of the time; joint custody was awarded in 15.5 percent of the cases. "In addition, the U.S. Census Bureau found in 1991 that fifty percent of all fathers involved in divorces didn't receive any court-ordered visitation."[70] In *Surviving the Breakup,* Wallerstein and Kelly note that half of the divorced mothers interviewed reported no value in the fathers' continuing relationship with the children.[71]

Maccoby and Mnookin found that of 1,000 divorcing couples in California, when both parents asked the court for sole custody, the mother received it 46 percent of the time and fathers were awarded sole custody less than 10 percent of the time.[72] Consistent with the tender years doctrinal belief mentioned earlier, if the mother asked for sole custody and the father for joint custody, sole custody was awarded to the mother 68 percent of the time.

Ellis points to the need for more specific guidelines for adjudicating custody hearings and the need to acknowledge human fallibility in the decision-making process. She recommends that statutes be revised to exclude "improper considerations by courts and expert witnesses, including conscious or unconscious gender biases."[73]

Maria Cancian and Daniel Meyer note that "understanding custody arrangements and the factors related to these trends is important for several reasons."[74] Studies can show what effect existing state custody laws have on shared parenting decisions and when and for whom these decisions are being ordered. Furthermore, Cancian and Meyer have inquired whether "changes in custody outcomes can indirectly indicate changes in family organization."[75]

Blumner stated that the best interests of the child standard requires reinterpretation. A new philosophical standard should, she contends, recognize "that the children's interests are no more important than the constitutional rights of both parents to actively rear them."[76] Artis corroborates in her research that judges using this standard actually "allow their inherent biases toward maternal nurturing to seep in."[77]

It may be assumed that legal decision-making affects or reflects personality characteristics. One's self-perception and behavior choices may be based upon the quality of the separation and the current household structure resulting from the parental separations. Therefore, let us proceed to examine these effects.

CHAPTER 2

———∿∿∿———

EFFECTS OF PARENTAL SEPARATION AND DIVORCE

EFFECTS ON CHILDREN

Children relate variously to their home parenting situations. Attorney and child advocate David Levy had for twenty years observed the negative effects of parent separation. He writes, "Perhaps 35 million children under age 18 at any one time are from divorced or never-married households. This increases poverty, ups the crime and drug rate, and produces school problems and unrealized accomplishments for many children and families. It also means that there are millions of noncustodial fathers and mothers—and grandparents—who are not fully part of their children's and grandchildren's lives."[78]

That many societal problems appear to be associated with the high rate of divorce and father absence suggests the need for further clinical research and examination. Particular efforts might be made by human service professionals to ascertain if these problems can be traced to parent separation. "Divorce is extremely stressful, but we usually regard stress as an adult problem. Children of divorce also experience high levels of stress but lack the coping skills and opportunity adults depend on."[79]

Psychologist Janet Eaton writes, "Pre-divorce communication and parenting styles, which frequently supported the parenting relationship, often became a serious source of post-divorce conflict."[80] Eaton's work suggests that child outcomes are directly related to the quality of the parents' relationship and the degree of their conflict.

Let's examine how parents react to family dismantling when parents separate.

EFFECTS ON PARENTS

Most parents separate with some degree of amicability or acceptance. They are able to navigate the transitions both inside the courtroom and outside within the newly defined relationships for child visitation and child support. However, nearly one-third of parents face these changes with great difficulty.

Parents tend to be quite fearful and face what many of them believe to be a perilous and, oftentimes, a fruitless effort for access to their children and their child's emotional investment. Yet many mothers and fathers fight to remain involved in the lives of their children. Lee interviewed more than one hundred children and concluded, "In most cases where the noncustodial parent claimed that visitation was blocked, it was true. While there were some instances where the interference was warranted, in many other circumstances the custodial parent had no justification for blocking visitation."[81]

Ahrons found that only 12 percent of divorced parents maintain a friendly relationship post-divorce. She found, too, that "fifty percent of middle class divorces maintain continuously highly conflicted relationships for at least five years following the divorce."[82] In their longitudinal study, Amato and Booth report that children are more vulnerable in "high conflict marriages that last and low conflict marriages that end in divorce."[83] Their findings indicate that low conflict marriages remain better for child outcomes than if parents divorce. It is only when parents separate from highly conflicted marriages that children show improved emotional and behavior outcomes.

Hetherington and Hagan find that "in response to divorce, depression, anxiety, emotional instability, irritability, impulsive behavior, and disruptions in identity as well as health problems associated with disrupted immune system functioning may occur in parents."[84] As parents harbor personal conflicts, both expressed and repressed, many children are victimized by the inability of parents to reasonably cope with their own anxieties.

Braver's research tells us that the most insidious degree of acrimony is during the time window beginning six months before and six months following parental divorce, which he refers to as the "emotional peak period." During this time, the acrimony between litigating parents takes its toll with verbal abuse, threats, and, indeed, violent incidents. Braver and O'Connell report that nearly 20 percent of husbands claim violent episodes in the home, whereas, nearly 30 percent of wives report such incidents.[85]

FAMILY VIOLENCE

At the onset of custody hearings, it is not uncommon for accusations of domestic violence to be made. "The courts usually take the position that even if the allegations are flimsy, it is better to be safe than sorry. And judges are taught that batterers are habitual deniers."[86] The courts are ready to protect individuals who fear another's anger expressed through threat, stalking, and prior physical abuses. Restraining orders are often quickly approved without hearings because the courts would rather err on the side of safety.

In this manner, a judge may seek to prevent harm by one parent against another. However, this is done by allying him or herself with the accuser, usually the custodial parent. Research psychologist Sanford Braver found that "even if the allegations are flimsy, [the accused] is rarely given the benefit of the doubt or assumed innocent until proven guilty beyond a reasonable doubt."[87] Sometimes, judges try to prevent the use of such allegations as legal tactics in custody hearings by warning of custody changes if the allegations prove false.

When allegations of family violence or fears of conflict ensue, it is usually during the initial litigation. Here, courts may order that psychological evaluations be conducted on each family member—parents and children—along with a cessation of any child contact by the noncustodial parent until evaluations are completed. Child access can be blocked for many months, upwards of six to eight months on average. "Generally, it is important that contact between the child and the rejected parent be maintained during the evaluation process. This serves two purposes: It enables the evaluator to obtain critical data about the parent-child relationship, and it might prevent further reinforcement of the child's rejection of the parent."[88]

In preparing interventions from both within and outside the court system, it would be useful to be able to identify potential abusers. Pagelow's research found several categories of people who might be capable of violence as follows:

1. those whose childhood homes had an abusive father and who mirrored the abusive behaviors;
2. those whose low self-esteem led them into bouts with sober violence or alcohol inducing violence;
3. those from traditional or machismo-type households ruled by male superiority, and
4. inexpressive individuals[89]

CULTURE AND CONFLICT

The Family Service Association of Toronto, Canada studied the Iranian immigrant population and found that "maladjustments" to Canadian life led to high conflict between the spouses and subsequent divorce.[90] Their data found that, as fear, cultural misunderstandings, and personal loss increased, household tensions escalated, to result in parental separations and subsequent divorce.

The Association found that during separation, husbands, particularly fathers, felt they lost standing in their community (neighborhood). Lost pride and manifestations of low self-esteem were common among them. Seldom was an extended family member or family support group available to console or otherwise aid one or the other or both parents. Highly conflicted divorces were most often found because of the frustrations due to language barriers and resources including advisory and professional support services.

Parents become impatient when the resolution of their problems was limited to a strict adherence to a lengthy, legal process. Indeed, the process is not limited by the day the judge issues orders. Further court appearances may be needed to deal with obstruction to child access, therapy, child support modifications, and other financial issues. "As a result, parents frequently set unrealistic expectations for themselves and their children and assume that their lives will be greatly improved in a matter of months. When these expectations are not met, frustration, anger, and disappointment become apparent."[91]

Parental Alienation

In the most extreme cases, parents exhibit hostile behavior, either overt or covert. They unconsciously or with forethought vilify the other parent—usually the absent parent—in the eyes of the children. Courtroom battling and domestic conflict cause children to feel insecure. "Children commonly interpret conflict as caused by the rejected parent and as abusive and victimizing of the aligned parent (and by extension, the child)."[92] This process is often described as alienation.

Given the high incidence of divorce, there is also a high probability of escalated or 'high' conflict evidencing the anger between the parents. Further, that divorce and custody are resolved through litigation in family courts, these angers are heightened, and the tactics used lead to greater tensions, and argument. This is not just 'theater', it is a horrific means for deciding the most tender of issues, parenting. This author has observed, read of and heard the testimony of vicious attacks used in the courtroom for child custody battles which utilize misinformation, exaggeration, and deceit.

When a parent is emotionally distraught, hurt and angry, as with others, it is not uncommon to for child brainwashing to occur. This brainwashing has been itself a source of argument by those who seek to demonstrate its presence and those who seek to deny its reality. Yet, this brainwashing, frequently referred to as parental alienation is common. Gardner, forensic psychiatrist and original researcher who labeled Parental Alienation Syndrome, or PAS defined it as "a disorder that arises primarily in the context of child-custody disputes. Its primary manifestation is the child's campaign of denigration of the parent, a campaign that has no justification. The disorder results from the combination of brainwashing, indoctrination by the alienating parent, and the child's own contributions to the vilification of the alienated parent." [93]

PAS poses a concept that confuses many professionals who find it too complex. Many attorneys argue that PAS and also PA cannot be reliably determined since neither condition is yet in the current edition of the *Diagnostic and Statistical Manual of Mental Disorders (DSM V)*. However, it is also argued by some that although the concept is not in the DSM as a diagnosis, its symptoms are and are characterized by emotional abuse, narcissism, bipolarity and borderline personality disorders. The courts frequently expect that forensic psychologists who interview and evaluate family members for custody and child access determinations will reliably testify as to mental health conditions of parents and children. The courts generally accept an evaluating psychologist's opinion in determining their own. However, psychologists differ in their interpretation of data. "Thus," writes Turkat, "the attorney attempting to assist a client by making a referral to a mental health practitioner in certain PAS cases may unwittingly be causing the client even more problems."[94]

A parent who believes their child is a victim of the other parent's alienating behavior must go to great lengths to demonstrate that PA or PAS is present. Review of state custody laws show that most parents who battle for custody must do so in a defensive posture. When the other parent objects to sharing custody, legal arguments become clouded with allegations. As cited earlier, accusations of child abuse, sexual misconduct, incapacity, and malfeasance dominate the arguments.

According to a study by Dunne and Hedrick, "PAS does not necessarily signify dysfunction in either the alienated parent or in the relationship between that parent and child. PAS appears to be primarily a function of the pathology of the alienating parent and that parent's relationship with the children."[95]

Determining whether alienation is present is complicated. It requires diagnosticians, i.e., forensic psychologists who specialize in identifying an alienated child and the source of alienation. "As in all child custody evaluation reports, the data that are relied on to form an opinion should be included."[96] Inclusion of this material helps show the perspective of the forensic therapist or other appointed evaluator. According to Lee and Olesen, "A failure to appropriately identify and intervene in the early stages of these cases may result in the alienating parent being given professional support for his/her position, reinforcing the child's need to maintain or expand complaints about the alienated parent."[97]

PARENTAL ADJUSTMENT TO TRAUMA

Anger is not an absolute predictor of outcomes. However, it is known as a human emotion that can, if not properly vented, lead to destructive actions. "Feelings—specifically anger—cannot make bad things happen. It is not the angry feeling that is dangerous but what people do because they feel angry."[98] Family members react to frustrations with the court process, oftentimes irrationally and violently, without contemplating their reaction and alternative behavior choices. Huffer refers to this as Legal Abuse Syndrome, or LAS. It is the anger and fear driven by increasing desperation, confusion, and hopelessness.[99] Huffer directly relates LAS to post-traumatic stress disorder and finds that courts appear unable to account for effects of the litigation process and the court culture suddenly imposed on a family to resolve marital problems. What of children's response to court orders affecting the family?

CHILD ADJUSTMENT TO TRAUMA

"Children's adjustment is associated with the quality of the parenting environment."[100] When parents express bitterness, children are deprived of the continuing focus they require developmentally. Hetherington and Hagen write, "Children need parents who are warm and supportive, communicative, responsive to their needs, exert firm, consistent control and positive discipline, and monitor their activities closely."[101]

Consider: "The divorced family is not a truncated version of the two-parent family. It is a different kind of family in which children feel less protected and less certain about their future than children in reasonably good intact families."[102]

The court's understanding of the impact on children when parents separate is revealed through family relations studies, attorneys who represent the children in court, or admitted psychological evaluations. A court's understanding needs to be clear because legal decisions may impact severely on children. But courts become quite troubled when high conflict divorce leads to accusations of PA and PAS. Judges do not know how to interpret it, but they more easily understand children's behavior. When high conflict divorce plagues the courtroom with custody argument, judges are often frustrated. They truly are seldom able to adequately if not appropriately deal with custody without reliance on therapeutic evaluations. They become equally distressed and even angry when there accusations that PAS may be occurring. This is why intervention and accountability needs to be further qualified, for the children are thus victims, if not the pawns in this dyadic tumult. Says Baker and Darnall, "studies have consistently documented that post divorce conflict– regardless of custody agreement–is associated with subsequent negative outcomes for children (Amato, 1994; Clawar & Rivlin, 1991; Ellis, 2000; Long, Slater, Forehand, & Fauber, 1988)."[103]

Children's response to their parents' divorce is based on their age, gender, temperament, intellectual development, and life's experience. But neither the children nor the parents or extended family members can well prepare for the parental separation process.

> "The divorce process is unpredictable. This is true from the beginning of litigation when children often have little understanding of what is occurring, and changes happen rapidly and episodically, to the final decision, after several court dates where the whole procedure is expected to end, it finally terminates, and most involved are surprised. Finally, the people involved are changed as a result of the process." [104]

In these polarized families, one often finds the development of warring camps where "Mom's camp and Dad's camp become peopled, even enmeshed, with other family members, teachers, therapists, and attorneys who may be urging and promoting the rejection process. It is important to assess whether these other players have been recruited by the parent or are taking the initiative themselves." [105]

Developmentally, children respond to parental conflict, parental absence, and parental divorce based upon their intellectual abilities to understand and their household experience. They (as well as other relatives and family friends) are likely to be powerless to control and influence the complex and painful family dismantling known as divorce. "The more sudden and unexpected the announcement, the more stressful the initial emotional reaction."[106] Yet no matter how well both parents explain the impending or immediate changes, "children are caught in this whirlwind of feelings and they can experience a wide range of emotions including guilt, shame, blame, low self-esteem, anger, confusion, sadness, worry and fear."[107]

"Social science research seems to have little direct influence on trial court judges; my interviews indicate that social science plays a very limited role in trial court judges' decisions about child custody. Judges remarked that they do not read social science research on a regular basis, although they do have some exposure through judicial conferences and expert witnesses."[108]

FATHER ABSENCE AND FATHER PRESENCE

Statistics find father absence to be extensive though stable since the 1990s. Using data from the 1998 U.S. Census Bureau, Paisley and Braver found that "27.5 percent of children under age 18 were residing with a single parent, usually a single mother (84.1 percent), and about 11 percent had a nonresident, divorced or separated father."[109] It may therefore be helpful to look at behavior and family dynamics post-parent separation in relation to the changed role of the father who is no longer resident in (the marital) or child's home.

"Support systems take on particular significance at times of crisis for children, especially when the crisis involves the disruption of the family structure."[110] Kelly and Wallerstein (especially Wallerstein's accounts through her longitudinal studies) have provided substantial evidence that children's resiliency to parental divorce is not a firm guarantee. They affirm the research of Hetherington and others asserting that children thrive when there is stability and warmth, security and comfort in the home, but not all at the cost of one parent's absence.

When parents separate, the noncustodial parent finds that access to children greatly changes. "In reality, many fathers are relegated to a restricted visitation/access schedule, designated as every other weekend. Thus, when compared with non divorced fathers, the structural barrier of the limited access arrangement means that divorced fathers will appear less involved on most behavioral indicators."[111]

Research is becoming clearer on the relationship of father absence to emotional pathologies and ill effects on children in such households.

A memo issued by the Department of Health and Human Services in 1996 stated that children in families with an absent father were subject to low self-esteem, juvenile crime, drug and alcohol abuse, teen pregnancy, and suicide. McNeely notes that even further back "a 1988 United States Department of Heath and Human Services study found that at every income level except the very highest (over fifty thousand dollars per year), children living with never-married mothers were more likely than their counterparts in two-parent families to have been expelled or suspended from schools, to display exceptional problems, and to engage in anti-social behavior."[112]

McLanahan found the impact on single-parent households actually do differ between white and minority households. She notes, "The effect of father absence is greater among Anglos, though overall rates of teen mothering are lower."[113] Additionally, McLanahan found teen pregnancies to be greatest, at 40 percent, for both African Americans and Hispanics, while for whites, the rate averaged below 10 percent. McLanahan contends that "father absence appears to hurt more educated white youth more," because "single motherhood is more common and perhaps more institutionalized in the African American and Hispanic communities." [114]

Amato and Gilbreth's 1999 meta-analysis found that a father's continued involvement (father presence) with his sons and daughters greatly contributed to the children's emotional well-being. An involved father, they concluded, provides "consistent emotional support, praises accomplishments, disciplines misbehavior and supports children's school engagement."[115]

Pedro-Carroll concluded that it was not necessarily the contact frequency between father and children. She found that "authoritative parenting and close emotional bonds between children and fathers serve as protective processes that are clearly in the best interests of children and should be fostered by interventions and policies."[116]

Similarly, Rohner suggests that it is not necessarily the frequency of child access, but instead, whether the child feels accepted or rejected by the parent. In his Parental Acceptance and Rejection Theory (PARTheory), Rohner states that "children's sense of emotional security and comfort tends to be dependent on the quality of their relationship with their parents."[117] His studies over thirty years across racial, ethnic, and socioeconomic strata confirm this. Based on his investigations internationally, he concludes, "Evidence from PARTheory research documents the fact that fathers' love-related behaviors often have as strong or even stronger implications for children's social-emotional development than do mothers' love-related behaviors."[118]

Sara McLanahan writes, "The differences between children in one and two-parent families are not so small as to be inconsequential, and there is fairly good evidence that father absence per se is responsible for at least some of them."[119] In particular, she found that the risk of teen birth for young women of single-parent households was 50 percent greater, or 33 percent compared to 21 percent for teens from two-parent homes. Additional aberrant activities are found among youth when their fathers, especially, are noticeably absent.

Gurian reports in "A Fine Young Man" a parallel between juvenile crime rates and single parenting. "American arrests for juvenile violent crime have increased by 600 percent over the last thirty years, the highest increase of any industrialized country. The rate of increase in juvenile criminality has now outpaced the rate of criminality in adults."[120]

Juvenile crime remains high with felonies increasing at an alarming rate, especially among younger female offenders. In 1967 just 13 percent of juvenile crimes were committed by females. In 2000 that rate more than doubled to 28 percent.[121] The majority of crimes committed by female juveniles were by fifteen- to seventeen-year-olds, while the majority of crimes committed by male juveniles were by sixteen- to seventeen-year-olds.[122]

Significantly, 39 percent of homicide victims murdered by juvenile females were family members. [123] Only 9 percent of homicide victims murdered by juvenile males were found to be family members.[124]

It may become clear to the reader that in addition to parents and children, society at large also bears social and financial burdens when parents separate. There exists, then, a compelling reason to further examine some significant community factors that have immediate influence upon children and parents.

CHILDREN AND PUBLIC SCHOOL

Children spend much if not most of their day in public school. Therefore, it is important to learn about student behavior patterns there, especially in light of increasingly violent and deadly crimes such as those our society first noted nationally in 2002 at Columbine High School. Statistics are not easily available that directly evaluate the impact on children of parental separations. For instance, I was unable to locate reputable findings linking academic achievement with father absence, divorce, or custody litigation. However, research studies do report significant child outcomes that ought to be addressed by boards of education.

According to Kalter and Rembar, 63 percent of today's public school children have some kind of psychological problem including anxiety, sadness, moodiness, phobias, and or depression.[125] Their study found that 56 percent of children fall behind in their studies and show poor grade results compared to their actual ability. Using her National Survey of Families and Households, McLanahan demonstrated that children of single-parent households would drop out of high school at a rate (31 percent) more than twice that of children from households where a parent had passed away.[126]

Wolchik's study, published in the *Journal of the American Medical Association (JAMA)*, confirmed Amato's observation that children externalize their problems.[127] Kalter and Rembar found that, indeed, 43 percent of children show aggressive behavior towards their parents.[128]

Amato concluded that divorce threatens a child's mental health over the long term.[129] It is clear that children need security and love in their home life and that the continuing parenting role by mom and dad should be protected by the courts, which should, at the same time, understand the upheaval that the parents themselves have been experiencing. Studies show that schools have difficulty addressing the complicated expressed and observed needs of anxious, depressed children from households where parents are disengaging or have disengaged. Yet studies show that a very great many children are managed with behavior modifying prescriptions.

BEHAVIOR MODIFYING PRESCRIPTIONS

Not only is it reported that children arrive at school medicated, but frequently, authorization is given to school nurses to administer these medications.

Research is just beginning to address the widespread use of such mood and behavior modifying pharmaceuticals as Ritalin and Adderall in public schools in spite of recent FDA concerns. New York University's Child Study Center reports that nationally, between 2 and 4 percent of public school children use these medications; but also reports that the use of such medications may be as high as four out of five public school children in some communities.[130] In African American neighborhoods, the reported rate of use is more than 15 percent, and the rate is even higher among whites, which may indicate that medical insurance is more readily available to them.

Dr. Nellie Fillippopoulos, neuropsychologist in West Hartford, Conn., noted that "children with ADHD [attention deficit hyperactivity disorder] often have more severe reactions to divorce because of the presence of the disorder."[131] Her support of prescription use is cautious and depends upon individual-case needs following appropriate diagnostic methodologies. Fillippopoulos pointed out that the "logistical complexity of divorce, custody, and child access cannot be causally associated with (diagnosed) physical conditions."[132]

Clinical psychologist Benjamin Garber, PhD, urges family law practitioners to closely examine children of divorce who may be exhibiting ADHD-like symptoms. The concern is that "what may appear to be a contributing factor to the divorce may actually represent something else: behaviors that are symptoms of the trauma of family conflicts."[133]

On the issue of causality, Chiriboga and Catron point out that "it is extremely rare, in fact, to encounter studies that do follow people from a point prior to marital separation. This is unfortunate, since without such studies it is nearly impossible to learn whether the physical and mental health risks associated with marital disruption represent consequences or themselves may have led to divorce in the first place." [134]

Klein, who had served as Director of the New York Child Study Center, has been reviewing area studies of pediatric pharmaceutical use and found that in Virginia doctors prescribe Adderall or Ritalin without much uniformity in their diagnoses.[135] Providing school nurses with the prescriptions allows schools to administer these medications based on the written ADD [attention deficit disorder] and ADHD diagnosis. However, the study also indicates that prescriptions are used for many differing behaviors. Klein found that "ADHD is the only childhood condition for which stimulants have FDA indicators. It is likely that these compounds are used in a broad spectrum of childhood dysfunctions, only one of which is ADHD."[136]

Studies show that cardiovascular disease, depression, and suicide are among the detrimental physical and mental effects of long-term use by children of such drugs as Ritalin. Professor Emeritus Samuel Epstein, MD, of the University of Illinois School of Public Health, finds that the incidence of childhood cancers has increased 35 percent over the last twenty years. He warns, "These risks are compounded by the availability of attention deficit prescriptions correlating to the increased use of the amphetamine-based Ritalin and Adderall without efforts to use alternative safe and effective procedures, notably behavior modification and biofeedback." [137]

So many children still arrive to school either medicated or requiring that these behavior modifying prescriptions be administered by authorized individuals as school nurses. But consider that, though there has been a dramatic increase in rates of divorce and single parenting in the past twenty-five years, these years have also been characterized by the use of these powerful behavior-modifying drugs and by lowered academic performance and increased juvenile crime rates. Might there be a correlation between these child behavior outcomes and the use of these pharmaceuticals? Indeed, might these child behaviors be a result of troubled households? Urging by the FDA since 2006 of more careful dispensing of these medications gives continued reason to hesitate before medically treating these symptoms.

Pfizer's medical director of Worldwide Safety for the Control of the Nervous System says that most medications including many for children are not based on (adequate) clinical research. "Unfortunately, psychology, especially child and adolescent psychiatry, lacks the sheer number of studies performed in other areas of medicine."[138]

Child welfare when parents separate is certainly a key consideration. There may be a (long) period of extreme emotions in a changed home environment. Therefore, it is reasonable to assume that controlling child depression and modifying disruptive, even dangerous, behavior or delimiting a child's classroom attention appear reasonable goals for treatment. But when so many children are being given ADHD or ADD labels, it may be logical to inquire about possible causes of these behaviors. Perhaps more information about the quality of the family environment will result in a more accurate diagnosis of a child's condition.

Treating a child's behavior symptoms either pharmacologically or non-medically may not prove to be effective long-term solutions to conflict between parents. I would strongly urge the review of the research literature for studies that show that great care needs to be applied when prescribing treatment for children who possess these negative behaviors.

CHAPTER 3

———~m~———

INTERVENTION THEORY: HOW TRADITION AND RESEARCH CAN EFFECTIVELY INTERSECT

THE CASE FOR NEW INTERVENTIONS

Forensic psychologist Kelly Zinna of Prince George's County, Md., recommends that a system be established early on in custody and access litigation to control for possible interruption of child access. "[The courts] must articulate clearly that visitation is important and ensure that there be no deviation of the schedule. The courts must make it early at the time of divorce so that the number one job is to make it a priority for the child to have a relationship with the other parent. This might be best accomplished when judges are conditioned to ask, 'what have you done to assure your child a relationship with the other parent?'"[139]

Prior discussion has shown the great emotional, psychological, and financial difficulties many parents encounter with the onset of divorce, custody, and visitation issues including the litigation process.

These issues affect different family members in unique ways. For children, the effects may become so intertwined that professionals can seldom isolate them. Says Buscaglia,

> "The language pathologist sees the child as a lisp or a stutter or a language problem; the occupational therapist sees him as a motoric muscular movement problem; the school psychologist sees him as a learning or emotional problem; the physical therapist sees him as a muscle problem; the neurologist sees him as a central nervous system disorder; the behaviorist sees him as a behavioral response; the reading consultant sees him as a perceptual problem; the school administrator sees him as an organizational problem; and the teacher sees him as an enigma and often even as a pain in the neck!"[140]

As noted earlier, bad child behaviors may indicate several years in advance that parents run the risk of separation or divorce. Therefore, increased professional collaborations with focus on child behaviors may be of great value. Jack Shonkoff, MD, of Brandeis University and chair of the National Scientific Council on the Developing Child states,

> "We need new strategies to enhance understanding and to build public will that transcends political partisanship and recognizes the complementary responsibilities of family, community, workplace, and government to promote the competence and well-being of young children. It is easier to deal with the behavior of children while they are in pre-K than when they are expelled from high school or imprisoned."[141]

Given these varied perspectives, it may be valuable to examine new modalities that allow for interdisciplinary family-professional collaborations.

HOLISTIC AND COMPLEMENTARY THEORY

Contemporary nursing education provides a unique model for holistic healing that includes four primary factors, *or personal spheres*: physical, emotional, spiritual, and intellectual. The late psychiatrist George Engel of the University of Rochester School of Medicine pioneered the basis for this holistic approach, which he termed "psychosomatic medicine."

Engel advanced this concept based upon studies with physician John Romano some fifty years ago. In 1977 Engel published his holistic theory incorporating bio-psychosocial treatment for the patient. "We are just as interested in what's going on at the family level as we are in what is going on at the cellular level," writes Romano. [142] "Engel championed his ideas not only as a scientific proposal, but also as a fundamental ideology that tried to reverse the dehumanization of medicine and disempowerment of patients." [143]

As shown earlier, the consequences of parent separation and divorce are numerous, complex, and complicated. Clearly, such traumas may lead to continuing negative psychological conditions and escalating hostile behaviors. Social systems may want to question an individual's ability to cope with many traumas that can occur when parents separate. Given the complexity and intertwining of emotions and behaviors, a holistic approach to treating family members may prove to be pragmatic.

New Zealand psychotherapist Natalie Fraser stated, "Health cuts now ensure that only clearly diagnosed people and substance abusers are treated or hospitalized. The social problems now have to be worked out with people who are not interested and often not knowledgeable about the issues." [144] Fraser found that improved family outcomes can be achieved with broader diagnoses and coordinated treatments. She found that interdisciplinary collaborations could provide effective outcome possibilities.

There are some difficulties with the cultural ideologies of traditional disciplines where the focus usually remains on the provider's licensed abilities. Professional practices generally exclude broadened intake/questionnaires or personal questioning. For instance, in "25 Years Later," physicians Borrell-Correio, Suchman, and Epstein found little adaptation of Engel's philosophy on holistic treatment in medicine or social services.[145]

When asked about her interest in assisting this writer's research, Anastasia Kovscek, MD, the 2001–2002 national chair of the American Medical Association's Student Action Committee for Humanism in Medicine, replied, "I would like to help you. Our projects are focused on relationships in medicine, well-being, and use of alternative medicine, namely in terms of what attitudes and behaviors amongst medical students (for our evaluative process of our programs) are. Not to say that these discussions do not come up, but we do not specifically address how family dynamics may be changed."[146] Yet Cohen writes, "Pediatricians are encouraged to be aware of behavioral changes in their patients that might be signals of family dysfunction so they can help parents and children understand and deal more positively with the issue."[147]

Doctors Borrell-Corrio, Suchman, and Epstein advise in their 2004 report that private practice physicians need to better understand their own biases such as race and gender; that they also need to better empathize with their patients. "Mindfulness—the habits of attentive observation, critical curiosity, informed flexibility, and presence—underlies the physician's ability to self-monitor, be vigilant, and respond with compassion."[148] With new information about their patient/client, are further professional collaborations possible?

When asked about collaborations, attorneys may point to the current role of collaborative law. Tesler states that the goal of collaborative law is "the shared belief by participants that it is in the best interests of parties and their families in typical family law matters to commit themselves to avoiding litigation."[149] Collaborative divorce is an increasing, though still a minor, procedure in divorce and custody agreements. Its success is also based on the willingness of the participants to reject hostile litigation and to focus on a compatible solution.

CURRENT CHALLENGES TO FAMILIES IN TRANSITION

As Bronfenbrenner states, families are "the most powerful, the most humane and by far the most economical system for building competence and character in children and adults."[150] For instance, appropriate behaviors, academic achievement, juvenile crime rate, self-esteem, literacy, and other socialization outcomes might be identified with family structure. Ultimately, it may be very helpful to associate such outcomes with family structure or levels of adaptations to new family structures. If we can relate positive outcomes to family characteristics post-parent separation and divorce, then family professionals can opt for more effective treatments through available medical and psychological interventions. The successful outcomes experienced by traditional and non-traditional family units should give pause to study their successes. Then, the dynamics, relationships, and values that foster these successes ought to be incorporated as models and protocols for healthy families of today.

Critical review of today's available support services shows that there are many programs; but they are disparate and difficult for courts and parents to locate. There is no singular clearinghouse or evaluative authority for referral to them. Wallerstein, Lewis, and Blakeslee write, "If we want to improve our divorce culture, we can begin with better services for families that are breaking up."[151]

CHAPTER 4

——〰——

THE HISTORICAL REALITIES OF FAMILY LITIGATION

Once we understand the current phenomena playing out in our home life, in our family court experiences, and given the American history of these dynamics, we can then accept the context of our life at this moment.

Then, and only then, can new paradigms can be considered for practical application and pilot studies. For instance, family professionals may then intervene before stressors become unmanageable, perhaps work in consort with other professionals in treatment, and find other protocols to improve child and parent outcomes. Family attorneys can work more closely together in resolving child custody by referring to the research literature, educating our judiciary. More will realize that the traditional courtroom is not the place for emotional, family disputes and instead, look to support unified courts and alternative procedures as mandated mediation for both resolution and healing of families injured by their transitional phase of separation and divorce processes.

Therefore, this chapter will address the historical context of family issues including marital discord and breakdown, with a focus on adjustments to family change. With this new understanding, I will relate findings to outcomes, and suggest new ways that professionals may collaborate across disciplines.

THE EMOTIONAL PERSPECTIVE: FROM MARRIAGE TO DIVORCE

Most marriages begin with attraction, love, and commitment. Divorce can come as a surprise, even though the family may be ripe for the cataclysm. A marriage may be undermined when one partner spends too much time at work, away from family, or when job stress and overwhelming financial obligations—perhaps for the new car or the new home—come to the fore. Individuals caught in the fray of daily living are often unaware of the impact that such strains have on marriage and child rearing.

Marriage and divorce are two poles of the relationship spectrum. Marriage is a legal contract binding two people together in a matrimonial and property partnership initially based on professed love, obligation, and/or commitment. It is an American cultural trait for two people who desire to be with one another to do so in marriage.

The 1992 U.S. Census found that the median length of marriage for women aged twenty-five to twenty-nine was just under three and a half years. Ten years later, the number of both men and women postponing marriage until the age of twenty-eight had increased, perhaps because of their fear of marital failure. Most likely this fear is also directly related to the increase in cohabitation outside of marriage, a fast-growing cultural phenomenon in America.[152] Estimates are that 60 percent of couples are cohabiting. Statistics show that cohabiting couples are less likely than married couples to stay together.

Emotional desires for one another, current and expected physical fulfillment, financial security, common interests, and sexual intimacy are among the reasons for marital unions. However, shared agendas for life partnerships change over time. Sometimes, ironically, the very reasons for the attraction between two people become the sources of discord and, ultimately, divorce. As Jeffrey Cottrell commented, "Perhaps the romantic notion we have of what married life should be like rather than what it is like is a key factor."[153] The number of divorced individuals grew from 3 percent in 1970 to 10 percent in 2002.

Admitting failure or breakdown in any relationship contributes to low self-esteem. One may feel victimized when one has embraced marriage as a serious commitment—"in sickness and in health, for better or for worse, as long as you both shall live." When parents separate and marriages dissolve, one parent (or both) leaves the marital home; the partners often fight over the rights to parent the children, and they argue over the payment of child support. Braver finds that the top seven issues that most divorcing parents must settle include

1. physical or residential custody;
2. legal custody;
3. visitation or access;
4. child support;
5. spousal support/alimony;
6. additional child financial needs, i.e., education, medical insurance, travel expenses; and
7. property and debt division.[154]

Resolving these issues is emotionally and financially draining. Considerable time is also required for court appearances. Pressures from work, neighbors, and friends can make matters worse.

Contrast divorce with marriage. Usually, the beginning of a marriage is marked by joy and fun with exciting moments of confident expectation for the future. On the other hand, divorce depletes energy and foments anger. It results in the depletion of personal savings and retirement funds to pay legal, psychological, and other divorce expenses. Parental anger may be expressed through subtly or overtly hostile behaviors, ranging from sly criticisms to nasty language, lies, and other abusive behaviors.

Divorce is the resulting contract which both enter into, sometimes with one or two feet dragging and usually with great anxiety due to the nature of public litigation. As the goal in litigation is for one to win or compromise less, fear of loss accompanies the process.

When a relationship breaks up, a partner may ask, "Why me?" The one surprised by a failed relationship, the "dumpee," may place the onus on the "dumper." But according to Fisher and Alberti, the emotionally healthy approach is to accept the loss. Letting go of such internalized questioning will permit an individual to focus on his or her own growth.[155]

Divorce recovery is relationship recovery. Rather than blaming the other for being "a bad choice" and the reason for the failed marriage, one needs to find a more positive approach. Fisher's method incorporates several stages, which include acknowledgement of the loss, coping with one's grief, and becoming more knowledgeable about one's personality, choices, strengths, and weaknesses. The goal for the parent should be twofold: first, through therapy or other means of self-examination, to accept what cannot be controlled and build on one's self-preservation and self-esteem; and, second, to determine how to raise the children post-divorce through co-parenting.

Presently, there are few agencies which combine intervention and support for families that are breaking up. No lists of books or other resources are handed out to moms and dads when they leave the court. There are no professional referrals—only court orders. The courts are for litigation, which often is labored and festering. Family court litigants —including moms, dads, grandparents, and children— seek out new relationships or seek to preserve old ones through a process involving many judicial parties. New social dynamics parallel the court processes where parents become visitors, where schedules become more significant and formalized. New realities about family and one's association with the changed family unit transition into the unexpected.

The divorce process can be seen as motions for different personal agendas and different priorities for the mother and for the father, for custody and for child access. Society's values are still interpreted through legal arguments, which many family advocates suggest are biased.

Gender bias ought not to be a part of court decision-making. But, as you're finding, it historically has been the case. The philosophical "nature or nurture" argument calls into question a male's ability to parent a child. Cannot either parent be taught skill sets? It is not enough to accept John Gray's conclusion that "men are from Mars, women are from Venus."[156] Nor is it enough to believe, as an elderly black woman told Smith, that "black women come from the earth and black men come from the moon."[157] Smith argues that black women are not grounded when their men lack the skills to communicate with their women. Black men, he finds, have difficulty measuring themselves against still-existent discriminatory standards—thus, their continuing low self-esteem. For many, these attitudes are inherited from their own dysfunctional childhood and family life.

In speaking of the African American experience, Smith writes, "The pressures of day-to-day life, financial concerns, and opposing viewpoints must still be overcome throughout the relationship. This tends to overshadow the initial feelings, and children are helpless to assist their parents who are supposed to provide safety for them. Lack of expressed love in the relationship can cause a small child to painfully assume responsibility for his parents' conflict. The social difficulties of surviving are particularly difficult for children in black families at a low socio-economic level. They may emulate their parents and, as adults, tend to experience the same painful series of events that occurred in their childhood. The cycle never seems to stop."[158]

Menninger's belief that "what children see at home, they will do to society" should become a societal mantra. It is as universal as the need for food and water. The confusion for children may lie with their possible misunderstanding of their own parents' behavior and the significance of that behavior. Parents don't often speak of the feelings that motivate their actions.

It is clear that children need security and love in their home life and that the parenting roles of moms and dads should be protected by the courts, which should also take into account the upheaval that the parents themselves have been experiencing. Consequences of parents' behavior need to be understood as well, for the behavior may be dictated by the parents' culture. Behavior choices are limited and based upon cultural norms and self-perceptions. These choices may be at odds with the predominant American culture and those permitted by courts of law. It is so difficult to assimilate a new culture's norms and more difficult to control one's reactions when they are driven by emotional responses to threat or anger. Often, responses are based on one's self-esteem.

How important is self-esteem? Therapists say that low self-esteem leads to codependence and to escape from responsibilities. The belief that one is incapable of achieving relationship harmony can lead to antipathy, jealousy, and hatred, which may be expressed in violence including assaults, murder, and suicide.

The choice for marriage or "partnership dissolution" (separation and divorce) are choices manifest in geography, economics, and expectations of the marriage partner. Similarly, one's choices reflect changes in power and control, income, threat, or rate of violence. The causes of divorce are complicated, considering what is known about diverse cultural values and one's individual inclination towards power, control, and expectation among different cultures.

Still, it may be that a major cause of family dysfunction including parent separations and marital breakdowns this author terms "benign neglect." Complacency about a relationship after the novelty of love has worn off can sometimes be blamed for parent separations. A sort of laziness often replaces the courteous, thoughtful, appreciative expressions of romantic love. Differing interests, priorities, even overwork, and value changes can also be factors.

In patriarchal America, men controlled marriages at least until the last bra was burned in the mid-sixties and the new liberated woman shared a toke with her man. The women's movement has prompted the formation of new public policies that encourage gender diversity in the workplace and equal opportunities for men and women. An overriding goal continues to be job promotion and equal pay for the same job functions whether performed by a man or a woman.

Status Quo for Litigating Parents

Separated mothers and fathers whom I have interviewed over the years reported that their own parents and close friends helped them cope with the marital, custody, and/or visitation crisis at hand through periodic emotional and oftentimes substantial financial assistance.

Emotional support from family and friends included validation for feelings and, frequently, alliances against the other parent. Financial aid generally was for immediate mortgage or rent, creditors, and other living expenses. Attorney fees, court-ordered psychological evaluations, and child support were among the more frequently sought kinds of support, often before one or the other spouse or cohabiting partner left the home.

When two working parents share the household, income is generally greater than if one parent works. When a parent is absent from the household, both parents suffer economically. The absent or non-custodial parent also struggles to provide child support while meeting his or her own survival needs. Clearly, economic stress is greatly heightened for both parents, though (nontaxable) child support payments offer some relief to the custodial parent.

Compounding the financial changes and associated fears of maintaining a familiar standard of living is the unnatural court process, which is intrusive and controlling.

Parents may have to wait weeks or months before court ordered psychological evaluations are completed and then provided to the court so that judges may then decide on schedules for child access. In the meantime, child access may be completely cut off or reduced to a couple of hours every other weekend with supervision. Moms and dads become sadder and angrier. Sides are drawn between Mom and Dad, who defend themselves and accuse each other of neglect, bad parenting, shameful behaviors, and manipulation of the children.

During depositions to the Connecticut Governor's Commission on Divorce, Custody and Children in 2002, several parents reported that their attorney told them it would cost a minimum of $25,000 to go to court to defend one's right to parent. Because the cost to litigate can run upwards of one thousand hours of billable time, many parents, whose only option is a trial, have surrendered their parenting rights. But these parents do not cease payment of child support, for to do so would land them in prison.

Fear, intimidation, and jealousy frequently play out in a relationship through argument, avoidance, and absenteeism. Domestic or family violence may erupt, a result of numerous frustrations and disappointments in the family dynamic for which interventions had either not been applied or poorly done.

High frustration levels are frequently exacerbated by required litigation. The exhaustive process for divorce, custody, child access, and child and other financial support are all usually conducted in the same manner as litigation over property and rights. Indeed, the cost to the litigant is both financial and emotional.

Those litigants who elect to represent themselves "pro se" are frequently viewed by opposing counsel and, indeed, the presiding judge as impediments to the court process or even as instigating parties bent on bringing their former partners to court as a punitive measure. But often, the pro se party is the one who could not afford to continue with a contracted attorney or who believes that results would be no better with an attorney on his or her payroll.

To quote retired California judge Donald B. King, "The role of the family law court too often is to shoot the survivors."[159]

To understand the nature of divorce, custody, and child access today, it will be necessary to put into perspective how our society has evolved over the last century, with respect to sociological and legal interconnections. Following that, we'll explore the possibilities for improving outcomes for children and their families.

THE HISTORICAL PERSPECTIVE OF CHILD CUSTODY

Child custody has emerged over the last hundred years as one of the most rancor-filled issues in our society. It concerns itself with the question of where the child shall live and who shall continue making decisions on behalf of the child. Issues regarding medical care, schooling, religion, and social activities are brought to family court for ultimate orders. Child advocates claim that awarding children to a primary parent and allowing for visitation or parenting time with the other is as inappropriate today as it was a hundred and more years ago.

In 1890 it was not uncommon for a divorcing mother to lose custody of her adolescent children to the father. Convention required that a labor-intensive agricultural society retain its self-sufficiency and economic survival. To maintain the family farm, which provided the family's sustenance, including income, it was necessary for children to stay at the marital home/farmhouse so that economic production would continue. The courts could not, therefore, interrupt what was the "backbone" of American life.

Regarding children and child welfare, in very recent years it has become clear that the presence of parents directly relates to the quality of life and the resources the child can access. In 1890 pregnant single women were closeted in regional "homes for women." The women were hidden from society and were not accounted for. Then, they represented a very small percentage of mothers. Today, teen mothers make up part of the single-parent households in which 24 percent of children under nineteen years old live. According to the 2000 U.S. Census, 68 percent of children live with both their biological parents, down from 77 percent two decades before. The census shows that 4 percent of children lived with their fathers and another 4 percent lived without a mother or father present. That means over 30 percent of school age children live in single-parent households today. It is reasonable to suppose then that one-third of all parents are noncustodial.

Geography has played a role in American marriage and divorce. Consider that, in continued western exploration, Indian wars, territory settlement, and the California Gold Rush—all stimulating opportunities for young and married men—took place in nineteenth-century America. In the young and free United States, American men, including many immigrants, eagerly sought new challenges and new prospects for finding income, building careers, and establishing homes. Many families were separated when husbands and fathers left to find new lives for their families and, for some, new lives for themselves. Consequently, these men left husbandly and parenting responsibilities. Falling out of love was not uncommon, nor was it difficult to hide one's marital status.

As Hartog explains, the federal government provided no uniformity of marital status accountability, leaving it up to each state and territory to legislate and enforce its own marriage culture and requirements. "States competed with each other for settlers: for the unhappily married, for the inadequately divorced, for those who wanted to marry or remarry. The marital regimes—the states— subscribe to rules (statutes) that each state has itself legislated, instituted and maintained using the courts and other institutions for the loyalty and tax dollars of a mobile citizenry. In that sense, diversity within the federal system was a simple product differentiation."[160]

Family law was in the throes of evolution. States introduced legislation that reflected the majority religious interests of their population (e.g., the strict settlement of domestic property disputes in Irish Catholic New York and Massachusetts, and the more liberal view of women's rights in the Protestant Midwestern states of Ohio, Michigan, and Wisconsin). It is interesting to note that the original legal acknowledgement of shared or joint custody occurred when, "in 1860, New York's legislature granted equal custodial rights over their children, if the father possessed no unobjectionable characteristics."[161] But the New York Supreme Court found it unconstitutional and ruled that "no rational legislature could have meant to divest fathers of their rights."[162] Yet most states' laws required that the woman's rights follow the law of the land wherein her husband resided. She also needed to be present in court in order to be heard.

Before 1860 there were legal arguments based on the father's right to his children's labor or custody, Following the Civil War, cases ensued that challenged the father's rights to sole custody, especially when very young children were present in a household. Testifying before the New York State legislature, suffragette leader Elizabeth

Cady Stanton stated, "In mercy, let us take care of ourselves, our property, our children, and our homes."[163] The effort was to find joint child custody a deserving role for both parents, with specific opportunity for a mother to nurture and raise young children who were dependent upon her. The custody rule drafted by New York was reversed as noted earlier. In New York in 1905, a boy "given" to his mother when he was of "tender" age would later, when he was older, be awarded to the father, since, the court advanced, the father had not given up any rights to his custody.

One hundred years ago, obtaining an education was difficult in many American landscapes. The agricultural communities of individual farming families could not easily sustain a school, let alone a salaried schoolteacher in a vast and unpopulated area. Compounding this problem was the unavailability of transportation technology to deliver children to and from school. Transit systems were limited. Children had to commute many miles by foot. Frequently, school days were structured around the labor needed on the family farm.

Until around 1915 and following divorce actions, the courts ordered custody of older siblings to their fathers, who needed their labor on the family farm. After that, courts began to award child custody (primary and sole custody) to mothers. This judicial selection for custody award was reversed at a rate paralleling the adoption of new technologies in the agricultural communities. It also seemed to parallel the rate of rural population migration to the increasingly densely populated urban cities and growing metropolitan areas.

From before the Civil War, the large cities of New York, Philadelphia, Houston, Chicago, Atlanta, St. Louis, and San Francisco had been absorbing large numbers of poor, uneducated immigrants fleeing persecution, hunger, and poverty from around the globe. These new migrants gravitated to the cities where they could easily find positions in growing manufacturing and service sectors of a new, diversified economy. As time and technology advanced, particularly after World War I, the largely agrarian American society embraced urbanization and its new culture.

Beginning in the 1930s, increased demands from diverse

populations called for changes in policy and departures from the status quo. Unions grew at a rapid rate, pressing for reforms with regard to safety, income, and equality. Owners/management grew ever more fearful of, and distanced from, labor over such issues as woman's rights, civil rights, occupational health, gay and lesbian fights for acceptance and equality, the rights of the mentally ill, the right to home school, the right to obtain an education. Conflicts over these issues continue, both in and out of court.

As America's urban and suburban neighborhoods have changed, so too have America's cultural values, especially since the 1950s. For instance, through the 1950s, marital rape and domestic violence allegations were excluded from many courtrooms where wives had sought refuge. The ideals of husband domination and family secrecy prevailed. All too often, headline news and "talking heads" sensationalized domestic problems, reporting on individual situations without placing them within a broad social context. Both the media and the public for whom the media speaks still frequently misunderstand the substance and outcomes of divorce and separation, which are well documented by contemporary family researchers. Negative stereotypes and profiling of fathers from all cultures and families continues: noncustodial parents, deadbeat dads, latchkey kids, and single parents. Correlate these labels to fathers' rights groups, incidents of domestic violence, restraining orders, stalking—and we have media attention and controversy.

From the 1950s through the present, there have been many changes within our legal system, including more statutes that are universally adopted by the various state legislatures. The liberal sexual mores of the 1970s, with the new availability (and acceptance) of birth control methods, encouraged modifications of family law. The tender years doctrine popularized in the early twentieth century was reborn as a policy of restricting child rearing to the mother—this, in spite of fathers becoming more engaged in nurturing their children. No fault divorce became more prevalent along with child custody awards to mothers.

The fact that women were increasingly pursuing careers,

controlling their own finances, and running for public office bolstered court arguments for equality of property and custody. Statistics show that in high conflict cases, judges have more often than not restricted a child's access to the noncustodial parent, (re)defining that parent's visitation to several prescribed hours during the week, alternate weekends, and occasional holidays. Judges generally assume that children will thrive best when raised by their mothers.

In over one hundred years family structures have changed as much as neighborhood environments. Each state has enacted laws to reflect the cultural norms of its constituents. Today, there is more mayoral and gubernatorial support for same sex unions as well as equally strong opposition to this perceived immorality. Interestingly, many of the states opposed to same sex marriage are those that do support civil union, reflecting their belief that partners in love may share financial benefits and child adoption, but that the marital union should be reserved for those who are able to procreate naturally.

States have reaffirmed their rights to decide matters of family law in spite of the threatened imposition of a federal definition of marriage. In 2004 the U.S. Senate was split on its support for a constitutional amendment ratifying the definition of marriage as solely between two people, one male and the other female. The same vote taken in April 2006 was defeated by greater numbers.

The increased vibrancy of these arguments, the cultural adaptations to new things American, and the development of new migrant communities are processes that repeat themselves as new immigrants come from the Soviet Union, Viet Nam, South America, India, the Middle East, and Eastern Europe. The American media and social institutions continue to expedite their adjustment to American culture while challenging their cultural values.

THE CHALLENGE OF CULTURE AND FAMILY VALUES

Culturally normal behaviors are those that reflect the values a society accepts as good, right, and appropriate. Marriage, divorce, domestic violence, and physical punishments are all behaviors that can be measured. Yet, as empirically sound as the numbers may be, they do not explain the cause of those behaviors or the values shared by differing people. Motivating behaviors may be more shared than not.

Cultural adaptation and cultural adoption are facilitated by the social service and educational systems that care for children in most communities. Head Start preschools, ESL (English as a second language) programs, and after school programs provide supplemental food, education, and other types of care for children. These programs accommodate households where either nutritional needs are not easily met or where parents cannot be at home because of work commitments. These programs are also intended to mainstream American cultural values. Communities fortunate enough to maintain such expensive programs do so in spite of nearly record numbers of budget cuts since the new millennium. A review of the mission and outcomes of these programs is outside the scope of this project, but such an examination by multiethnic, new immigrant, and interracial panels might prove quite revealing.

Without investigating the American cultural ethos in all its manifestations, it may be reasonable to claim that the United States has struggled with an emerging national identity. The country has grappled with international leadership and respect while coping with issues of new legal and illegal immigration. Our national identity now embraces varied ethnicities, which dominate in various industrial, political, and economic sectors.

American cities have evolved since the emancipation in the 1860s. With the close of World War II, poor African American populations have come north since 1945. Their children have struggled against racial barriers and a dearth of educational resources. As one generation moved away after education and income attainment, others moved in. In some intensely urban communities, illegal and legal migrants from Hispanic America have moved in. Where largely single-parent households once dominated, now various young Hispanic families have set up homes with numerous single men or women and families sharing apartments.

Cultural norms differ from one community to another. The neighborhoods of New York City's Lower East Side, Chinatown, Harlem, Little Italy, Wooster Street, Delancey Street, Amsterdam Avenue, and 181st Street call to mind certain colors, sounds, and sights that are unique and representative of the people living there.

The reader may wonder how discussion of cultural norms relates to court intervention in divorce and custody matters. But consider how our immigrant grandparents and great-grandparents might have viewed divorce. Was divorce an acceptable alternative to faithful Catholics? Was it a right of a husband to divorce a seemingly barren spouse? (Indeed, a woman who could not conceive was disgraced.)

The choices of love and hate are not always expressed the same way or to the same degree. These choices are culturally unique to such American subcultures as African American, white, Hispanic, Asian, and Native American. Though there are many other subgroups, particularly as the rate of immigration increases, it is easier to compare the larger categories named above. It may be helpful to consider power and conflict in these groups.

Lucy Rios, Director of Prevention and Communication for the Rhode Island Coalition on Domestic Violence once revealed to me that "culture and religion impede the goals of less conflicted and more amiable parent separations."[164] Rios also found that immigrants from non-Western countries, particularly those countries that were patriarchal or male dominated suffered more when their cultural and or religious values clashed with the more liberal, Western society advancing gender equality and opportunity. This cultural clash is further exacerbated through easy access by the more inquisitive and younger immigrants of the American internet, TV and other media.

For instance, a communal leader who doesn't speak any English cannot readily assist an immigrant with economic, legal, or socialization challenges. The immigrant with questions is compelled to seek answers outside the community, for example, from the police.

But whereas police may be a source of protection, an immigrant may also feel afraid of the uniformed "men in blue."

Contemporary American society supports egalitarian opportunities. But consider that Latino cultures tend to be patriarchal. A young Latina who dreams of college and a scientific vocation will face cultural obstacles to the fulfillment of her dreams. They have become Americanized. Their values are now those of the adopted homeland.

Illegal immigrants face new fears of unemployment and of extradition and deportation. Rios recounted that court interpreters are not always skillful and available, so that immigrants may remain unaware of choices that would be more acceptable to the American way of living and their rights to make those choices.

Those immigrants who are without family support face additional challenges. They must rely upon others who may be ethnically similar but who themselves have very different or changed attitudes about child rearing, housekeeping, work, and language. The challenges for the courts are to a) understand cultural norms and expectations, b) explain how they are in conflict with American law; and c) make rulings that are clear, judicious, and compassionate.

Behavior of those inside a culture may be misinterpreted by those outside it, as Rohner implies in the following passage: "In cross-cultural and multiethnic research, however, one must attempt to view the word *anger* as being descriptive of parents' behavior, not judgmental or evaluative. This is so because parents in about 25 percent of the world's societies behave in ways that are consistent with the definition of rejection given here (Rohner, 1975; Rohner and Rohner, 1980), but in the great majority of cases—including historically in the United States—these parents behave toward their children the way they believe good, responsible parents should behave, as defined by cultural norms."[165]

Clearly, cultural differences may be poorly understood by those outside a value based population. Cultural norms within a household with respect to habits, routine, food, and behavior including child rearing can be so complicated and foreign to the outside observer that family court judgments may be based on misinformation and ignorance of cultural motivations.

Identified cultural communities will function best with cultural ambassadors who can mediate between the ethnic community and the American community at large. Police departments use such representatives to influence gang behavior. Similarly, training by local community-based "ambassadors" may provide effective interventions in family and related matters including juvenile and probate court.

It is simplistic to refer to American culture as though there is uniformity from one neighborhood to the next. America today still retains great diversity within many communities. The liberated woman we see in today's boardrooms, newsrooms, and dental and law practices had parents who supported her choices. But, today, there are also women of other cultures who remain less emancipated than American advertisements and TV shows suggest.

For instance, Southeast Asian Hmong congregate in various regions of the country, yet continue to live their traditional family structure.[166] Hmong mothers nurture their children, focus on the raising of the daughters, and defer the decisions of the nuclear and extended family members to the dominant father.

Similarly, Hispanic men dominate their families. Though Hispanic women are generally becoming more assertive, like their American counterparts, it is the Mexican women who have become the most assertive. Mexican women earn as much or more than their husbands or other male family members. The women send money back to their Mexican families to help raise their standard of living in Mexico, or they use the money to help finance other family members' travel to the U.S. Because they have been more successful than the male day laborers in earning money, the women have wrested power away from the traditionally more controlling and powerful males.

As women obtain financial parity and control, their role as providers gives them more family power. Such a challenge to power, though, is not acceptable within other Hispanic cultures. Puerto Rican women continue to face domestic violence, sometimes by mates resentful of their women's ability to be self-supporting. The machismo of the Puerto Rican male suffers when the weaker sex becomes more financially autonomous.

"As the relationship becomes more serious, the issue of control becomes more important and violence is likely to occur."[167] The dynamics of control are evident in the use of physical and psychological abuse that can be conscious or unconscious, voluntary or involuntary.[168] Oftentimes, physical and psychological tactics are interwoven, and they occur at seemingly spontaneous times when there is particular vulnerability or when the results will be most predictable.

It is urgent when discussing abuse to identify who is capable of violent behavior. Domestic violence crosses socioeconomic and cultural categories. When the batterer feels cornered, hopeless, or seeks to obtain and solidify family control, then emotional and physical abuse becomes likely. Low self-esteem exacerbates these feelings. They may also lead to drinking and illicit drug taking. Such behaviors can become habit forming over time and indeed may lead to actions that are illogical and dangerous.

Wallace says that physical or emotional abuse may occur in 16 percent of marriages. But others find in their review of Department of Justice data that the rates of abuse are more than double for those who are unmarried.[169] While it can be argued that divorce might prove to benefit all family members, statistics show that marriage offers more protection from abusive relationships. Still, for many, divorce or separation of the parents would be less painful than the continuing rounds of verbal and physical sparring between them. Indeed, physical separation might prove to be a practical survival mechanism.

One reason that cohabiting couples may experience more incidents of abuse is that there is no support system for them. There is no established nuclear family, in-laws, or extended family. Tending to be younger than married couples, such couples often exhibit immature and irresponsible behaviors in response to lack of a support system, economic stress, and inability to cope with responsibilities such as those that teenage pregnancies bring.

Youth, inexperience, and the inability to communicate well can be a frightful, combustible set of factors that add to the fragility of relationships. The successes of Mexican women, the self-sufficiency of African American mothers, and the efforts of better educated Puerto Rican women are assets for a couple or a family. Nevertheless, for many males these "assets" threaten their own sense of purpose as breadwinners and as knowledgeable decision makers. The sense of threat may be so overwhelming that it leads to violence.

Unemployment or underemployment can predispose someone to inflict injury. It seems that such facts, if documented in a client folder, might be helpful in subsequent discussions with family members as a means of thwarting potential incidents of domestic violence.

Professionals schooled in mainstream white culture with an Anglo understanding of behavior are likely to believe that family violence is caused by psychopathological reasoning. Yet many cultures are distinctly *not* of mainstream American culture, nor do they innately possess its values. An understanding of cultural norms can guide the practitioner when working within different cultural communities having regular interaction between mainstream American and other community leaders. Such efforts may be more effective in conveying a clearer understanding of behavior expectations.

Professionals with such cultural understanding will also be able to help clients anticipate the consequences of choices that may be acceptable within their traditional culture but which will run afoul of the American legal system. Perhaps a study of majority populations would help minority populations. "Black family life appears to be a precursor of what family life is likely to become for the rest of the population. While African-American families undoubtedly face some stresses that are unique to them, they are instructively viewed as prematurely suffering the negative consequences of an American family environment that all groups share."[170] Unchecked, the aberrations of our minority communities may become more endemic to other populations.

The use of the court system for changing lives now follows. This system needs to be examined for its current processes, impacts, and potential to help all families.

COURT AND CULTURAL SENSITIVITY

Litigants in family courtrooms around the country have observed widely varying responses by judges presiding over cases that address child custody, child access, and professional testimony on shared parenting. Each court is autonomous in its "culture," as defined by the presiding judge. The cultural differences are expressed by the judge's demeanor and by his or her consistency or inconsistency in communicating with litigants based on their gender, race, and ethnicity.

I observed a female child-support magistrate admonishing a parent, "Sir, I don't care if you have to pick up bottles and cans, *you will* continue paying your child support."[171]

The same judge heard a young, black father proudly announce that he had "gone straight" in recent years after having served time in prison as an adolescent. He excitedly interrupted the judge several times, proudly boasting that in spite of odds, that he had started a small painting business and "changed" into a more mature man; he had grown wiser and more responsible. He argued that he had become a legitimate businessman, practical in his personal financial management, dedicated to and focused on his work. The judge seemed unimpressed to hear, to understand the man's achievements.

I held back tears. I wanted to embrace him, to congratulate him.

Yet, despite the man's earnest, "Yes, Your Honor," the court magistrate appeared to grow more cynical, more impatient. She told the man to begin paying down his arrearage in child support. The judge did not want to hear about the success this individual had had in overcoming the inner city street culture I envisaged had him trapped for some thirty years. The judge gave no words to acknowledge the great steps this man had made to compete with white-owned businesses, to make an honest living, to change his life. The judge, perhaps overwhelmed with other cases, had no patience for this man's declaration, and cut him off without any further acknowledgement.

It is a cultural tragedy when a judge or magistrate sits on the bench, high above the courtroom crowd, and seemingly far from the litigating parties standing below at their respective tables. A judge's caseload imposes upon him or her the need to attend to the issues at hand as speedily as possible in order that other cases may be heard within a specified time period. The job requires decisiveness. But it can be argued that a heavy judicial caseload, coupled with individual predispositions, prejudices, and cultural misunderstandings, can preclude statements that opposing litigants need to make at a hearing and prevent adequate deliberation.

It may be that justices need a framework, a new format in which they can more actively participate in the case before them. Such a framework might permit the judge to more clearly "hear" what is being said and to understand the motivations behind the messages being delivered. Such a framework may help to empower the litigant seeking validation for what is right and to understand what is wrong. The judge may also feel more empowered in his or her role of providing guidance as well as justice to both litigating parties.

At a meeting of the local bar association in Silver Spring, Maryland, an African American attorney stated emphatically that "when judges sit on the bench and tell these parents they have a responsibility, then we'll see more couples behaving themselves and doing the right thing."[172] He explained that he was raised in the rural South, a region where, he said, there was more respect for children than he had found in Maryland.

Nationally, what is "the right thing" for custody determination is not dictated by federal law. Family law is unique to each state. Let us now look at some new interpretations as well as conflicting viewpoints.

CURRENT REALITIES OF LITIGATION

Court procedures for resolving family issues are extremely costly for stressed parents, with legal fees as high as several hundred dollars per hour of service. Attorney fees for a court appearance may include billable time for preparation and waiting time while in the courtroom. A motion for *pendente lite* (initial separation agreement) can incur twenty or more hours of attorney fees, which is why lawyers usually require new clients to provide a retainer (prepayment) of five to ten thousand dollars. Modification of child support can itself take five to ten billable hours, given the need for current income documents for one or both parties, discussions with accountants about tax consequences, and other supporting evidence.

Attorneys have a seemingly laborious and detailed duty to follow the procedural requirements for case filing and documentation, to prepare for their court appearance, and to serve their client maximally. Their knowledge of the law is impressive to the litigant who puts their full faith and trust in their legal representative. That trust is one that may blind a party, since the average litigant does not understand court methods nor can they anticipate outcomes. Yet, it is such an understanding and clear goal of the litigant which will make it easier for them to comply with the systematic process of forensic evaluations, family relations studies, and appointment of attorneys.

Throughout the litigation process, attorneys may be hired to provide a voice for the minor children (Attorneys for the Minor Children) or to serve as case advisors to the court (Guardians *Ad Litem*) recommending what they believe is best for the minor children. A valuable element in custody litigation, findings are yet argued, with additional challenges over which therapist shall evaluate family members and under what circumstances noncustodial parents may see their children. So it is not always decipherable in whose interest litigation is for. After all, it is the attorney's role to win in behalf of their client. Should it not be that the 'win' be the goal, but instead, that the children's best interest standard be the focus for court? Questions remain as to whether litigation is a reasonable means of settling custody.

CHILD CUSTODY AND LITIGATION

Custody has been mentioned throughout this document since it is endemic to the family court system and the source of many parenting issues when parents separate.

According to the American Bar Association web site, seven of the fifty states do not provide specific authorization for joint custody.[173] These seven states without a legal statute authorizing or supporting joint custody include three from the conservative, deep southern states of Alabama, Arkansas, and Georgia; the two Dakotas of the western region; and conservative and religious West Virginia. It is notable that the perceived liberal state of New York has awarded sole custody more frequently to mothers than other states, in spite of requests for joint custody considerations going back to suffragette leader Elizabeth Cady Stanton.

The rub in this analysis is presumptive powers. The presumption that both parents will share custody when they divorce is a feature in most state laws. However, this feature is not interpreted uniformly in those states. For instance, family courts in just twelve states uphold joint custody at the onset of divorce.

Eight states recognize joint custody as being optimal, but only if both parents agree. What this demonstrates is that in spite of joint custody being favored in most states, it may still remain a point of litigation between two parents.

A significant consideration in joint custody decisions is the burden of proof. If a parent objects to the other's sharing custody, then the question again remains as to who must present evidence for or against shared custody. In most states, this burden of proof is on the accused defendant parent, usually the noncustodial, to show why he should retain shared custody.

A recent California ruling upheld basic concepts of a child's rights to be accessible to both parents following parent separation, but not without an opposing viewpoint.

The California Supreme Court ruled in April 2004 that a primary (custodial) parent cannot relocate out of state with the children "so far that would preclude them from having an on-going relationship with the noncustodial parent."[174] The California Women's Law Center called the California Supreme Court's ruling "a huge step backwards" and demanded that new legislation be issued that would assure the custodial parent's assumed rights to move out of state with the children.[175] In its verdict, the court motioned that

> the [appellate] court was correct that the situation might have been far different had the parents shown a history of cooperative parenting. If that had been the case, it might have appeared more likely that the detrimental effects of the proposed move on the children's relationship with their father could have been ameliorated by the mother's efforts to foster and encourage frequent, positive contact between the children and the father. But the court reasonably concluded that the present case presented the opposite situation.[176]

In 1998 Cynthia McNeely wrote, "If the treatment that fathers receive in family court occurred in the workplace, an affirmative action plan would likely be implemented to rectify the pervasive discrimination and barriers fathers encounter as they seek meaningful access to their children."[177]

In the *St. Petersburg Times*, an article addressing "Court Ordered Sexism" reported that the National Organization for Women (NOW) government relations director issued a memorandum denouncing "men's custody groups such as the Children's Rights Council because they aid non custodial dads in reducing their child support obligations and in taking away custody from moms."[178]

Groups like NOW and domestic violence organizations have fought against the rights of children to two parents post-divorce when the mother voices opposition to joint custody or shared parenting. In 1996 NOW adopted a resolution at the annual conference which asserted,

> WHEREAS organizations advocating "fathers rights" whose members consist of noncustodial parents, their attorneys and their allies, are a growing force in our country; and WHEREAS the objectives of these groups are to increase restrictions and limits on custodial parents' rights and to decrease child support obligations of noncustodial parents by using the abuse of power in order to control in the same fashion as do batterers.[179]

A seminal time in American jurisprudence requires a judicious view of the needs of children. For instance, the NOW Preamble contains the following text:

> WHEREAS many judges and attorneys are still biased against women and fathers are awarded custody 70 percent of the time when they seek it per the Association of Child Enforcement support (ACES).[180]

The preceding gives reason for women's rights, but the statements lack context, understanding statistics of current court custody decisions. It appears defensive and represents what to some is a backlash to the histrionics of child custody awards when mothers were given sole custody.

Ideally, child custody arrangements should not be arbitrarily assigned. Novinson urges courts to compel child access orders including the provision that custodial parents be accountable. He further suggests that custodial parents who interfere with child access be punished by the court. He further advocates that "improper parental influence (is) awarding custody ... to the candidate who is more willing to foster the child's good relationship with the other parent."[181]

Yet the conundrum is how to determine what is in the child's best interests. Though resolving the problem of child placement (custody) between parents has been redefined through the years, there are at present no uniform standards for court decrees and family laws. The children's best interests standard is more of a colloquial standard, subject to individual interpretation, than an external barometer or baseline for assessing family behavior and outcomes.

Fathers not subject to allegations of abuse and fathers seeking to preserve their roles in raising their children continue to be viewed by many family courts as obnoxious and vexing. This is particularly the case if they represent themselves in court (pro se). Yet fathers seeking an active role as noncustodial parents are doing what is natural—namely, protecting their children from intrusive, external elements threatening to change the father's role to that of a visitor at best and a nonentity at worst.

In the family courtroom, attorneys trained in litigation procedures dutifully argue their clients' rights as they might in civil or criminal courtrooms. Is the family courtroom the most appropriate place for resolving marital dissolution and custody changes?

Many hearings for restraining orders, contempt charges, and abuse allegations have been used as tactics to delay custody findings or to bring more favorable custody outcomes for a pleading parent. Court hearings have been used to determine appropriate access to children and schedules for visitation with them. Let us take a look at the nature of child access (visitation) today.

LITIGATION AND CHILD ACCESS (VISITATION)

"Visitation is understood to be one of the most critical factors for families involved with a child welfare system and it is the quality of the visitation that is most informing with respect to the case plan goals and overall permanency planning for children and families."[182]

When parents separate, perhaps the largest "bone of contention" is the nature of the relationship of each parent to his or her child. Research increasingly documents that children have developmental and behavioral needs for two loving parents beyond the parental splits. The continued relationship between the noncustodial parent and their child is increasingly referred to in the professional literature as 'child access' rather than the oft used 'visitation' an archaic misnomer, still found in many states' custody statutes, parenting agreements and other documents.

'Visitation' is the pervading legal term, which reflects for moms and dads when and how often they may interact with their children. 'Visitation' is documented through court order or other agreement, defining when—the days and times—that a mother or father can be a parent and also determines the limits of their parenting authority.

The fact that courts intrude upon the lives of families in decisions of custody and access angers many parents who are unfamiliar with the judicial process and uncomfortable with court formalities and slow processing time. Based on many observations in New England courts and those in metropolitan Washington, DC I have made the following conclusions. A litigant's anxiety is often due to lack of experience with the litigation process, which in turn colors that person's perception of any hired counsel. Clients may view their attorneys as superficial in spite of reassurances. Additionally, clients frequently see their attorneys jockeying representation between several other clients and showing inattention and impatience in that process. The greatest problem for litigants is that little is explained to them about their court experience, which leaves them uncertain of the process. Attorneys also tend not to share their knowledge of research about shared parenting, visitation, and the effects on families of continuing hostility between parents. Nor are they known to offer resources or refer to support groups.

The notion that resolving child custody and child access is urgent for the parents is typically not reflected by what they perceive as tedious motions, slow case scheduling, laborious legal procedures, the litigious legal process. Parents are still identified as the defendant and the plaintiff. The "he said, she said" arguments would best be replaced with child-focused discussions referring to current research on shared parenting and child access and alternatives to the frightening, punitive, and aggressive litigation process.

Terminology is a significant factor when helping people, namely parents, through divorce and access matters. A noncustodial parent resents his labels as a "visitor" when his commitment, based on love and desire for nurturing, remains as a parent, not a guest. A noncustodial parent has to struggle continually against the "visitor" role, fearing that they will eventually perceive themselves as a visitor or non parent. Such self recognition, is not the intention of the court, however, it may morph the parent into an estranged role when engaging their child during a scheduled time sharing (visitation). With such a perspective, the parent may become agitated, fearful, and angered. For some, they may subsequently assume an inappropriate, assertive behavior that is uncharacteristic, and possibly dangerous, all which presents frustration and torment.

The self-perception had by such a 'visitor' is reinforced through the sociological phenomenon known as the "looking glass effect." It takes its name from the story of *Alice in Wonderland,* which contains the powerful notion that an individual can become what they believe others perceive them to be. Whether mom or dad, the noncustodial parent is viewed as a part-time parent or visitor who has to negotiate with the primary parent the when, where, and how of seeing his or her child.

"At its core, the visiting relationship is ambiguous and therefore stressful. A visiting parent is a parent without *portfolio.* He lacks a clear definition of his responsibility or authority. He often feels unneeded, cut off from the day to day issues in the child's life that provides the continuing agenda of the parent-child relationship."[183]

This is interesting when one considers that the matter of child support is not easily debated. Instead, child support is based on state formulas that determine each parent's portion of monetary contributions for raising their children.

Among the first national child advocates to raise the fact that child support includes both financial resources and emotional capacity was Attorney David Levy, a founder of the Children's Rights Council in Washington, D.C. In 1985 Levy found that child access, that is, the continuing relationships with child and the noncustodial parent (mom or dad), is the 'cornerstone right' of a child to more assuredly achieve emotional health and physical well-being.

Levy advocated the research which demonstrated the link between child access and payment of child support. Through his office on Capitol Hill, Levy promoted new research and spearheaded the publication of new findings on child outcomes and shared parenting which were often in contradiction to accepted principals and state statutes in family law.

Through his public speaking, and consultations with Senators, Congressmen, and the White House officials, Levy was able in 1996 to bring this concept to the attention of then-Federal Commissioner for Child Support Enforcement, Judge David Gray Ross. Ross acknowledged the need for continued parenting by both parents post-divorce. Ross brought this message to state offices of child support through redesigned newsletter logos and Department of Health and Human Services departmental meetings. Ross agreed with the Children's Rights Council mantra, "The Best Parent is BOTH Parents," a statement coined by attorney Michael Oddendino, cofounder of the Children's Rights Council.

Following the election of President George W. Bush in 2000, I had the pleasure of meeting with Sherry Heller, then the incoming Commissioner for Child Support Enforcement of the Federal Department of Health and Human Services. In that meeting with Levy and Teresa Kaiser, then-Maryland Executive Director for Child Support Enforcement, Heller affirmed her belief that child support was both financial and emotional as her predecessor had accepted.

Four years later, poster images of involved fathers graced the walls of many child support agencies. However, there has been essentially little 'trickle down effect' of this message, this acknowledgement that parents mattered, and were more than a checkbook. In most of the child support offices I had visited in different states for the Children's Rights Council, I found glass barriers remained to separate visitors—no messages of emotional support for parents and no signs that caseworkers can help with other needs and referrals such as therapy, employment, and retraining. Indeed, caseworkers are seldom assigned to individual parents for the long term; nor do they offer themselves as resource people.

If child support is more than financial, then one would expect these child support agencies to deal with more than financial matters. But parents often learn about child support services when behind in child support or when accused of methodically underpaying or ignoring court orders for child support.

That courts continue to bifurcate (separate) financial child support from emotional child support requirements including child access is indeed an unfortunate situation. The data above show this. Yet, if one could measure a child's ability to weather her parents' immediate separation and divorce (child resiliency), one would discover the importance of socioeconomic factors including personality and household interactions prior to the parental split. They might be used as quantitative measures to be compared to affective outcomes from court orders or other benchmarks. In this way, cases that would ordinarily return to family courts might instead be routed to a monitor within the court's family relations department for further counseling.

Divorce and child access struggles are particularly debilitating both emotionally and financially. Those obligated to use the court system must cope with so much that is unfamiliar, threatening, and seemingly insurmountable. It can be crippling to those acting pro se, choosing to represent themselves in court instead of hiring paid counsel. The power wielded by the consummate decision maker, the family court judge, and the mystical measures of one's attorney are greatly intimidating. The court has often been described by family law attorneys and parent litigants as a veritable "minefield."

The court's attempts to focus on observed case symptoms rather than underlying causes has traumatic results. In his or her ruling, a judge may set aside the recommendations of court family relations investigations and even court ordered forensic psychological evaluations—this, in spite of the fact the judge may have no formal education in family dynamics or training in psychotherapy. New attorneys and new judges may themselves be a product of divorce and single parenting. It would be interesting to study such judicial members and their custody decisions.

As litigation provides ample opportunity to exploit the weaker, sometimes unrepresented, parent, then access to children becomes a fight. The primary or custodial parent usually retains control of the child's activities and religious participation. It is also easy for the custodial parent to limit telephone access and visitation with excuses such as "Johnny isn't here" or "Beth is sick" or "Tommy doesn't want to see you now." Often, as the divorce process ensues, primary parents have the opportunity to brainwash their children with repetitive statements, such as "we don't need him, we don't love him, we don't want him." Children's emotions are easily "held hostage" or manipulated by a controlling parent. Some clinicians have historically held that "children know the truth." But sometimes children know only the truth they are told by the parent upon whom they depend for food, clothing, and shelter.

The issue of one parent denigrating the noncustodial or absent parent has been difficult to fight in many courtrooms. Court motions brought by the noncustodial parent to subvert alienation are generally poorly handled by the courts. In spite of the severely negative outcomes that such parental alienation may upon bring a child, courts bicker over reasons for the alienation. The courts question whether alienation has resulted from a maliciously conceived action of the primary parent or if it is simply the reaction of an angry child. Attorneys are also known to debate the issue of parental alienation as to whether it is a child's own manifestation or whether it is manifested deliberately by a parent and consequently identified as parental alienation syndrome (PAS). Was the child taught to hate the other parent or are the child's feelings based on the child's own perceptions?

Yet attempts by the court to intervene are few and, when implemented, tend to be too late. Successful alienation is long term and harmful, even dangerous. The fact that alienation is often the result of brainwashing necessitates a protocol for deprogramming. It is that severe. Consider that despite their opportunity for freedom with prisoner exchange and the end of hostilities, more than forty Korean-era American servicemen remained in North Korea. Several hundred servicemen are reputed to be remaining in Vietnamese cities and hamlets. The point begs the question that if adults can be so irreversibly brainwashed, could it not be that children, with developing and immature minds, are even more susceptible to brainwashing?

Observations show that hard-pressed noncustodial parents do not easily receive a sensitive ear from many family judges and family law attorneys. Busy dockets do not permit the time to listen intently for some understanding of the alienated parent. Many litigants seek a compassionate ear through clergy, therapists, friends, and family. Others write letters to editors, join support groups, and search web sites for answers. More proactive parents, eager for legal and legislative information, seek membership in shared parenting advocacy groups, such as Levy's DC based Children's Rights Council, Ned Holstein's Boston based National Parent Organization (formerly Fathers and Families), the Texas based Parental Alienation Awareness Organization and the DC based American Coalition for Fathers and Children.

Desperate, activist parents seek media attention, hoping to find a compassionate public ear and an equitable (and rapid) remedy for their situation. They seek sympathy and, often with the support of new intimate partners, they argue, demonstrate, and vociferously advocate for change in state and public policy.

Family Structure and Public Policy

The new millennium has only recently begun, bringing a new census data-gathering effort. Trends for divorce, single parenting, grandparents raising children, and blended or stepfamilies, as outlined in sociology texts, are now becoming acceptable statistical realities in most parts of this nation. The rate of divorce remains high and predictable. Single parenting remains the rule in most urban areas. Single, teenage mothers nearly outnumber households where parents cohabit.

Where there are children, there are fathers and mothers who are obligated by court order to assist financially with child support. Many teen dads and others, particularly those unemployed and underemployed, do not pay the child support, leaving many single mother households vulnerable to poverty and its ills.

Consider such recent welfare legislation as the Tax Reform Act of 1996. This is one of the first laws provided by the Temporary Assistance for Needy Families (TANF) program that places a time cap on benefits for welfare recipients. The TANF renewal (scheduled for 2004) was expected to provide marriage incentives for low-income people. Said Wade Horn, former assistant secretary for Health and Human Services (HHS), "We're basically doing three things. The first thing we're doing—through various demonstration authorities—is we are taking a look at the integration of marriage education services into various public sector service delivery systems. For example ... the Refugee Resettlement Program."[184] It is interesting to point out here that TANF federal funds are awarded as block grants to each state to provide funding for welfare recipients. These funds are provided with the expectation that each recipient state will aggressively identify and collect child support payments that remain uncollected.

The federal government has also provided that as more and more people owing child support obtained jobs and could pay their support, then the TANF funds could be now be used by the states to provide more social services that are also family strengthening.

But Horn, above, references use of these TANF dollars for immigrant families since "the stress of being a refugee and coming to a foreign culture often provides enormous stress on marriages. And that they (the refugees) thought it would be helpful if we were to provide, on a voluntary basis, access to marriage education services for those refugee families who think it might be helpful to them as they adjust to a new culture, *and the stresses and challenges that that reflects.*"[185]

The Federal Department of Health and Human Services has sought the means through demonstration projects to try to save "fragile families"—refugee couples—and also to encourage low-income people to strengthen their marriage, and to encourage low-income, unmarried parents to get married. The department reflected upon the following federal birth statistics and trends to examine how public policy might need to readdress education, welfare (TANF) programs, and public policy.[186]

Statistically, the number of children living with a single parent is rising for all major American ethnic and racial groups. In the early 1960s, the rate of out-of-wedlock teen births for African American girls was 51 percent, whereas for white teenagers it was 12 percent. In the early 1990s unmarried white teen mothers constituted over 50 percent of births. In 1960, 22 percent of black children lived with a single parent;

in 1990, 20 percent of white children were living with a single parent. Yet consider this: in 1997, 75 percent of white children lived with two parents while only 35 percent of African American children did so. Fewer than 65 percent of Hispanic children lived with two parents. Viewing these statistics another way, consider that approximately one quarter of children live with their mothers, 4 percent with just their fathers, and 4 percent don't live with either parent.[187]

According to Cancian and Meyer, "If fathers provide more resources to their children when their children are in their custody, then a trend toward shared custody has important implications for the resources available to children."[188]

Levy concurs with the federal government that father absence leads to less family income and lowered health outcomes for many children and that "much remains to be done in the U.S., but all 50 states recognize joint custody, and in 26 states and Washington, D.C., it is only a presumption or preference."[189] These rather strong findings ought to be further evaluated so that family law might be reexamined in the interests of improved outcomes for children. Public policy initiatives that formalize support for continued two-parent involvement in children's lives can be strengthened.

The above research shows several significant effects of father absence. In spite of the correlation of negative outcomes with father absence, little is done in family courts to assure children of their rights for two parents post-divorce. Existing joint custody statutes offer little protection for children in many family courts when justices freely interpret custody and child access (visitation) statutes and frequently impose their own rulings with immunity. Though statistical logic and social reasoning support that father presence ought to be enforced, the very lack of court enforcement of child access (visitation) orders may contribute to frustration by the noncustodial father and encourage father absence.

Levy, who had studied joint custody and shared parenting since 1985, found that the issues of child access and custody throughout the United States are similarly debated in other Western countries. He found that the noncustodial father relationship is the most frequently occurring post-divorce dynamic and as many as 500,000 children—nearly 50 percent of those from divorcing households annually—lose contact with their fathers. Nearly 40 percent of noncustodial U.K. fathers lose contact with their children shortly after divorce.[190] That noncustodial fathers lose contact with their children is not unique to the U.K.; it is a statistically significant fact in many Western countries.

Australia was one country that sought to correct this. In December 2003 the government of Australia introduced the Australian Families Tribunal with the goal to reduce adversarial resolution of child access and custody. It sought a means for separating parents to spend less time in litigation and thereby incur a reduction in legal expenses.

DADS of Australia and the Shared Parenting Council of Australia lobbied for a presumption that a child's parents should share equally the responsibilities of child rearing and residential custody. The Australian parliament's bipartisan Family Services Committee recommended legislation to support parents' sharing in major decision making on behalf of their children (joint legal custody) but would not recommend equal access (referred to as fifty-fifty shared parenting) for their children. Then in 2005 the Australian legislature passed a federal law mandating that shared parenting be the presumption for divorcing parents with an effective date of July 1, 2006.[191] The Italian government issued a similar national law in 2006.

The aforementioned actions suggest a universal right of children to two parents. Families without two parents are families at risk. The point being so strongly made here is that children do best when both parents remain involved in their nurturing. Given that sole and residential custody awards are still usually given to mothers, let us discuss how the matter of parenting remains a matter of civil rights.

SHARED PARENTING AND ENFORCEMENT: A MATTER OF CIVIL RIGHTS

The 1950s and 1960s civil rights movement for racial equality has similarities with the struggle by fathers and mothers in family court for the right to preserve their role as parents during and after parent separations and divorces. The juggernaut of family court is inhibiting and frightful to the many uninitiated to judicial procedures and family litigation. The judicial maze takes a great emotional toll on litigating parents. It also places a huge financial burden on those seeking protection of their parenting rights post-separation and divorce. Given these difficulties and challenges to all parties, it is conceivable for one to ask, should court processes consider changes for dealing with family issues of custody and parenting? Might family members be better protected with changes in public policy?

This latter question was asked of Jack Greenberg, one of the leading attorneys to bring the lawsuit of Brown v. the Topeka, Kans., Board of Education to the federal superior court.[192] This pivotal case in 1954 concluded by striking down segregation in America's public school systems. Attorney Greenberg was asked how courts could affect changes in public policy. He replied that courts can (a) set a standard, (b) set an impetus, and (c) "prevent bad things from happening" through the use of punishment guidelines. Ultimately, Greenberg stated, there was "no single approach to a problem."[193]

Family advocates consider the issue of children and parents' rights to be a matter of civil rights, especially when parents decide to separate. Therefore, Greenberg's discussion of civil rights, law, and public policy remain significant to this day. It is reasonable to assume that the successful education and advocacy methods of the civil rights movement have been adopted by constituencies seeking to preserve family relationships when parents elect to separate or divorce.

Since 1985, the struggles to overturn perceived gender bigotry in family court determinations led to rapid creation of national organizations of parents and also grandparents. These organizations lobbied state legislatures, held public demonstrations for joint custody, and supported the social research examining divorce rates, custody assignments, high conflict divorce and child outcomes.

Organizations as the David Levy's Children's Rights Council, Nate Holstein's Fathers and Families (now National Parents Organization), Julie and Jean Castagno's Grandparents and Children Embrace Inc.,

Wendy Perry's Parent Alienation Awareness Organization – all have offered support to parents feeling estranged from the legal process, and to educate the judiciary on matters of joint custody. Their mission includes advocating for children to be raised by two parents who may no longer live with each other and to assure children continuing relationships with grandparents and other extended family members.

The suggestion of gender bias has been examined since 1985, and found necessary to consider as mothers were most frequently awarded sole or physical custody. The extent of custody decisions favoring mothers prior to the last several years has mirrored that of racial bias and segregation. It is therefore highly important to examine the similarities between gender (or parent) bias in the courts and that of racial discrimination as these decisions likewise mirror social norms, if not values. Then, it will be significant to consider why advocacy for parenting rights be considered similarly.

The federal action against school segregation resulted in the overturning of the "separate but equal" doctrine. This doctrine states that schools serving black students are to provide the same learning opportunities as those schools serving predominantly white students.

The separate but equal doctrine provided for racial differentiation and continuing barriers between those of different skin color. Greenberg's comments above reflect the great opportunities that still remain for courts today.

The preservation of human rights remains the standard for family courts. Just as race, nationality, and skin color are theoretically invisible in the courtroom today, gender should be not be a factor in family court. Are not the needs of children such that they thrive best with two parents involved in their life? We have seen the federal statistics for children raised by single parents. The statistics show that children suffer great harm when a father is absent from their lives. As with preserving racial equality under the law, the goal in family court may be similar—to preserve opportunities to parent with love and guidance as well as to assure the continuing relationships between two populations—parents and children.

The successes of Greenberg (white and Jewish) and his co-counsel,

Thurgood Marshall (black and Christian), who represented the NAACP's interest in Brown v. Board of Education, preceded the federal civil rights legislation that was signed into law some ten years later. It was a lengthy process to obtain rights to racially integrate— rights to guarantee the same life options for African Americans as for whites. The enforcement of those rights also led to opposition from states whose majorities preferred status quo segregation.

In spite of its democratic underpinnings, the U.S. is not immune to cultural conflict when there is cultural change. The civil rights movement was characterized by education, confrontation, and policy change. The movement was emotionally charged and highly conflicted, but it tried to unite people of diverse and hardened opinion. Yet it was the courts of law led by the federal government that provided rules, order, philosophy, guidelines, and control of the population.

When considering family law statutes—their interpretation, their enforcement, and their need for change—representatives in both the house and the senate universally defer to the state legislatures. The states each have their own legislative histories and set of laws that reflect the cultural values of their respective populations. The federal government essentially allows states separate judicial powers for establishing and modifying state laws. Still, a federal proclamation in support of shared parenting or joint custody may provide guidelines for protecting the interests of both parents as fragile populations.

The need for federal jurisdictions and state protections continue to blur as society becomes more complex, as evidenced by the consolidation of departments under the control of Homeland Security. The state referendums in 2004–2005 for same sex marriage, assisted suicide, and eminent domain challenged federal law. State judicial court districts have proven themselves the most easily accessible for conflict resolution. Litigants usually have courts available within a short commuting distance, and court appearances are scheduled within weeks rather than months. Yet litigation usually is based on one or more motions, with hearings for those who cannot negotiate outside of court.

FAMILY OUTCOMES, BEHAVIOR, AND PREDICTION

As families become marginalized through separation, divorce, rejection (for some teens who become pregnant), dysfunction and role breakdown can occur rapidly and dramatically. Certainly, such families become predisposed to increased economic risk and aberrant social behaviors.

Earlier research may help explain which child behaviors suggest predisposition to household dysfunction and why child behaviors need to be monitored for the sake of family health.

In 1986 a study by Block and Gjerde found that "as many as 11 years prior to their parents' divorce, children from eventually separating families showed more behavior problems than children from always married families. Boys whose parents would later separate demonstrated a pattern of problematic behaviors at ages 3, 4, and 7, including a lack of impulse control, stubbornness, and restlessness. Girls from eventually separating families only had increased behavior problems at age 4 when compared to their peers who would remain in two-parent homes."[194]

Let us consider a fundamental problem and a fundamental solution to help us prepare for envisioning new interventions when families transition through parental separations.

In that the litigation process further divides parents and positions them as adversaries, children will continue to be victimized. As previously noted, social science research continues to confirm a plethora of negative outcomes, which require societal attention.

Outcomes for children may be expected to improve when each parent continues to function post-separation and divorce in roles that are complementary and communicative. Outcomes for children and their parents have a better chance for improvement when all potential negative effects on children and parents are known and when influencing or causal factors can be linked. With such knowledge, societal systems as the courts, educational system, and even penal systems may create alternatives for resolving and custody and child access issues.

It would not be unreasonable to presume that successful outcomes will be forthcoming when there are reasons and guidelines for increasing co-parenting opportunities and for enforcing court-ordered decisions. Professionals so enlightened and willing will be significant leaders in helping families to survive parental breakup.

PART II

THE FUTURE: BRIDGING THE PAST WITH THE PRESENT HISTORICAL PERSPECTIVES AND NEW PARADIGMS FOR FAMILY HEALING

PART II

"You can't always get what you want
But if you try sometimes you just might find
You get what you need"
The Rolling Stones, 1968

CHAPTER 5

—⟋⟍⟍⟋—

EMERGING POSSIBILITIES
FOR IMPROVING
CHILD OUTCOMES

FAMILY PROFESSIONALS: NEW AGENTS
OF POSITIVE CHANGE

"The truth of it is that so often we professionals tend to see children as their externally manifested bits and pieces. We tend to divide up. We tend to see each other, also, as *our* bits and pieces, instead of our external whole."[195] Leo Buscaglia, professional educator and brilliant lover of life, expressed that those working with children perceive them through their own unique magnifying glass.

As is true about each of our experiences, observations, and evaluations, what we perceive is based on our own view of the world. Professionals, no less, perceive similarly albeit through their own set of skills.

Understanding how these professionals serve individual family members will allow for a more complete review of their potential for intervention. Interventions may include the obtaining of more detailed data upon client intake, which might in turn reveal a client's needs for additional human service and professional referrals. Experience and professional training may also enable these agents to provide expanded help through professional collaborations.

Also helpful to families and a source for learning helpful interventions are the family professionals in training (FPT): graduate students in such professional and academic programs as clinical social work, psychology and psychotherapy, law, and school guidance counseling. These students often administer services to families through university-based training programs, outreach, and reduced-fee or free programs to qualified families and family members.

There are great opportunities for helping those with failing or disintegrating marriages. The many and varied observers of these families can observe the signs and communicate them directly to the family and/or to other appropriate professionals. These observers are the family professionals (FP), those who form the first line of defense, those with the most immediate opportunities to influence families. They include members of the medical and mental health fields, attorneys and legal advocates, educators, clergy, employers, educators, and family relations caseworkers. They also include those who presently work as licensed caregivers in helping professionals and allied fields.

Those who make first level of contact with family members may be considered primary family professionals. Those who have less frequent contact may be considered the second line of "family defense," and they may be referred to as secondary family professionals. Understanding their vital role in serving families and recognizing their distinct association with families is key to defining how they may effectively collaborate in preserving the health and viability of families post-parent separation.

I would identify the FP who engages families with parental stress issues as comprising the first and second lines of "family defense," since they are in direct and frequent contact with family members. They are all change agents who can effect positive changes in the contemporary family. State courts, state departments of Children,

Youth and Family; Social Services; and Child Support Enforcement are additional change agents when parents seek formal assistance with the issues above.

Society can empower children, tomorrow's leaders, by investing in broadened family-needs training. When the FP can identify those families where marital and parent partnerships are broken down, then individual family members can be targeted for special help including referrals to other family professionals. It may be argued that schools, the workplace, and the church may be better empowered as settings in which children and parents can be informed and given new skills for improving the family dynamic. Onsite resources can help families in transition cope with their changed dynamics through information, and medical and even clinical assistance. Those going through change seek acknowledgement of their transformations at home, recognition that these transformations may be burdensome, and help to manage their transitions optimally.

For example, an empowered school that can intervene when insolent or quiet children are identified as unhappy might prevent bad behavior including peer violence. If the school learns of a pending divorce, the school can consider options to assist the child in coping. When the school might do this without awaiting the parent's approval, then the assistance will be more immediate and thus more effective in thwarting any negative conditioning that is taking place at home.

What is being suggested here is a best practices approach to assisting families. Let us look to empower each family professional within a systems context. The literature shows that all court members and such FPs as therapists, clergy, and medical practitioners need to learn more about divorce dynamics and understand the developmental needs of children including their needs for two loving parents. It may be found, then, that better outcomes for family members will occur when family professionals are taught how they can implement effective and objective protocols when assisting families. They must also recognize the many emotional and financial transitions that may accompany these proceedings.

If we note Bronfenbrenner's Ecological Systems theory, we will find that family members are subject to numerous household (internal) and environmental (external) influences. These influences intersect and therefore the opportunities for professional collaborations present themselves. The collaborations are represented at the points of contact on any depiction of Bronfenbrenner's model diagram. These points of contact are what I would term 'vantage points'— logical areas for intervention and treatment both within the family and juxtaposed just outside the family's inner boundaries.

Both the FP and the family professional in training (FPT) can intervene, offering mothers, fathers and children struggling through their transitions of divorce and family change. The actions, opinions, and decisions of the FP and FPT will have long lasting or permanent effects on the parents, children, and extended family members.

Professionals working with families can effect immediate and long lasting changes for their clients. If professionals examine the broader implications of their client's current family situation, then they may offer more effective interventions. Professionals cannot claim that America's diversity issues relate solely to Hispanic, African American, Caucasian, and Asian subgroups. The U.S. has continued to reflect greater differences than census data indicate, particularly since World War II. Residing in many urban American areas are significant populations of first- and second-generation immigrants who have come (legally and illegally) from Mexico, the Near East, Eastern Europe, the Middle East, Africa, and South America. As these new immigrant populations become settled and adapted to the American systems, they also become stressed by their efforts to understand financial, social, and emotional processes.

In some state court systems, it is enough that Spanish-language materials are offered; but seldom does one encounter a bilingual attorney specializing in matrimonial and family law. Family professionals who speak only English and families with limited English proficiency are impeded in their efforts to navigate the legal system and to obtain mental health support. The increased tension at home due to a parent's helplessness further compounds the children's struggles to understand their parents' plight.

The FP and FPT will greatly benefit by incorporating into their practices a better understanding of how clients are affected by other professional and social influences. In professional life, one becomes an expert in a particular field; but there are few opportunities to explore related fields. It is a problem, however, that judges and matrimonial attorneys are not also students of psychology and family therapy, let alone sociology. Paraphrasing social theorist Abraham Maslow, Buscaglia writes, "If the only tool you have is a hammer, you tend to treat everything as if it were a nail."[196]

If we as professionals can question our own observations of clients' behaviors and understand their perspectives, then we will find more complete answers; we will demonstrate the interrelationships between external and home environments and clients' strengths and potential for transitioning well. More effective, comprehensive protocols can then be proposed and administered.

Let us consider how we might provide family professionals with a larger set of tools and options for helping families heal. Let us consider why and how we can improve family outcomes by improving skill sets for both parents and family professionals.

HOLISTIC PROTOCOLS

"Healing is a journey: a conscious realization that the choices made in this life, to bridge the soul and ego's separation, is the thread and strength of wellness."[197]

In order for these processes to be successful, there needs to be an articulated understanding of both child development theory and family systems. The factors that affect the family member and the family unit may be broken down into four life spheres, or circles, which connect with one another much like the international Olympics logo. The circles can be used to visually represent the interconnectivity of being, thinking, and behaving. Based on Engel's theory, these spheres include:

1. the *intellectual,* or "road knowledge," sphere—the practical information taught or emanating from learned experience;
2. the *emotional* sphere, which confirms our feelings, values, and behaviors;
3. the *physical* sphere, which provides a barometer of how well our bodies function and need to function for physical health and sustenance;
4. the *spiritual* sphere—that component which today is upstaged by cravings for videos, material goods, and play.[198]

As the front-line troops attest, there are no agnostics in times of trauma and foreboding. The spiritual self is the component necessary for validating one's existence with purpose, hope, and renewal. A child has no less a concept of self than an adult, whether articulated and demonstrated or not. Indeed, adults carry their formative years as their "inner child" and may behave later in life based on the realities of their youth.

The individual and family systems are complex as are their healing needs. Said Gaydos, "Human life is not simple; therefore, treatment need not be simple."[199] To treat an individual's ailments, one must begin with appropriate diagnostic methods. The challenge is to do so in an industry-regulated manner so that expenses can be recouped. Dossey identified the greater challenge: "If medicine is administered to treat symptoms, then there remains potential for the symptoms to recur. Though expedient to treat symptoms, the underlying cause for the symptoms remain. Therefore the question remains as to which are the most cost effective treatments."[200]

The contemporary theory of holistic nursing was developed in the 1980s and represents a wonderful view of treating individuals in change. The theory is based on a bio-psycho-social-spiritual model and acknowledges that patient health care has a psychosomatic component with four factors contributing to patient symptomology and treatment.[201] Those factors are: (a) biological, (b) psychological, (c) sociological, and (d) spiritual.

Each factor needs to be addressed when caring for an individual patient because the factors interweave uniquely for each person. As Dossey said, "The bio-psycho-social-spiritual model provides the major overall road map in caring for the whole patient."[202]

According to the Patient Bill of Rights, patient care cannot exclude any of the above factors. It states: "The provision of patient care reflects consideration of the patient as an individual with personal value and belief systems that impact upon his/her attitude and response to the care that is provided by the organization."[203]

Discussions with individuals including physicians characterize the above as an idealized mission. Parents interviewed over the last several years have reported that visits to their physician's office were characterized by routine, often impersonal and few questions instead of, *"When did you first notice this condition? For how long have you treated it? How are you treating this condition now?"*

Essentially, the delivery of American health care today appears to be standardized and brief. Though blood, cardio, and other tests might be ordered, their evaluations and conclusions are often hastily conveyed by an office nurse or other assistant and usually over the telephone. An overburdened medical practitioner may be relieved to have this assistance, but the patient may not feel personally attended to. Surely, medical diagnoses and remedies cannot be adequately provided given lack of sufficient data.

The holistic healing model—the model that is increasingly accepted by nursing administrators for nursing care—is most readily applied to hospitalized patients. It was the physicians that allocated little time to understanding the individual patient's physical and emotional state. Sloan wrote, "It soon became apparent that scientifically trained physicians, well versed in quickly and impersonally treating patients with acute illnesses, were not accustomed to treating personal and emotional problems associated with patients having long-term chronic ailments."[204] A patient so afflicted remains fragile and at risk. Therefore, she requires more detailed and complicated in-patient services for treatment as through surgery, chemotherapy, and other invasive protocols. Such patients may need additional services to accelerate healing and reduce the likelihood of physical complications.

This holistic model may provide a more comfortable transition to a new set of realities. Consider whether the time of hospitalization is the time to introduce holism. Might there be alternative interventions for treatment to prevent the desperate physical conditions necessitating hospitalization? Perhaps one's general practitioner might have prevented some conditions from necessitating hospitalization. It might be that, had additional questions been asked at intake, answers provided by the client may have allowed for earlier and more effective interventions.

For instance, what if, at intake, the patient/client were asked the following questions:

> "How are you feeling today? Why do you think so?"
> "How much alcohol do you consuming daily? Weekly?
> "Are you using drugs for recreation? How often?"
> "What drugs or medications are you taking?"
> "Do you get frequent headaches or heart palpitations? When?"
> "Are you feeling more anxious lately?"
> "Do you have difficulty sleeping?"
> "Are you sleeping too much or too little?"
> "Are you eating more or less than usual?"
> "Have you lost pleasure in things that you once used to enjoy?"
> "Do you often feel that life is not worth living?"
> "Are you spending more or less money than usual?"
> "Are you gambling or shopping more than usual?"
> "How are your children, spouse, and other family members?"
> "Are you content with your work?"
> "Have you been on vacation recently?"
> "Is the recession affecting you?"
> "Do you get angry easily?"
> "Do you notice any mood swings?"
> "Is your weight fluctuating?"
> "How are you doing in school?"
> "How is your love life?"
> "Are you exercising?"
> "Do you make time for hobbies? What are they?"
> "How much rest are you averaging each night?"
> "How frequently do you awaken during the night? Why?"

How would the reader answer these questions? Is the reader conscious of his or her answers to these questions? Indeed, how would the reader *react* if asked many of these questions by his or her health or other family professional?

No doubt, most of us would be floored, surprised, and mystified should we be asked these questions by a physician or a friend. These are questions that may seem so personal and therefore unexpected if heard from others. Yet we might dare ask ourselves several of these. Such a thorough survey of our physical condition might help us organize related symptoms and identify their causes. The survey might help identify a physical and/or emotional condition and suggest helpful interventions. The goal is to understand a patient's current physical and emotional state and to ascertain the means to influence the process of healing.

The process of collecting information needs to be addressed. Let us consider the challenges of professional data intake at point of service.

INTAKE

We associate "intake" with the assessment of changes in individuals' behavior or health. Intake data is also based on one's own admissions rather than professionally observed and recorded data. Based on the individual's disclosures, professionals select certain protocols for further diagnosis and treatment. It may also be that such choices depend on the individual's available health insurance.

In the case of divorce and related matters, the physician's office might offer referrals for psychotherapy and self-help including support for grief and loss. An over-riding goal for health providers is to maximize the client's potential for short and long-term recovery. For this change in the intake process to become an acceptable part of client interviews, there must be advocacy for it.

Consider this situation: A child injures herself in a fall from a swing at her school. Medical examination determines that a physical therapist is needed.

Questions: How often does the physical therapist speak with the educator who found that the child had fallen off the swing? Could the pediatrician have asked how high the swing was, why the child was on the swing, what time the accident occurred, how much experience the child had with the playground equipment, how fast the child was swinging, and whether the child was permitted to use the swing at that time?

Is there a responsibility to ask such questions? Is there a responsibility to share the answers? Indeed, could there be lessons learned from this incident to improve child safety on the school grounds?

If these types of questions were to be answered, then new behavior guidelines or protocols could be designed to reduce the likelihood of similar incidents. Based on understanding of the answers, interventions could be devised to prevent potential injury to children below certain heights, designated ages, physical abilities, or emotional conditions.

Practical monitoring of the children on the playground will reduce the potential for injury. Such monitoring would prove most effective if teachers and administrators with playground duties were trained to identify the children at risk. They could obtain or prepare instructions for shielding these children from the dangers of inappropriate swings. They could also provide referral procedures to classroom teachers who could then share any behavioral concerns with school psychologists or parents and guardians who would be in a position to intervene.

The above is meant to show how practical concerns for child safety can be implemented based on child's observed behavior choices through existing school protocols and the provision of professional intervention.

The initial client intake varies in length from professional practice to professional practice. Sometimes, it allows for a new patient to outline his perceived medical record and sometimes it includes family medical histories extending to parents and grandparents. But seldom do questions elicit more details about workplace exposures, hobbies, avocations, and habits. There is also seldom space on the intake form to identify personal concerns and marital problems. One will often find a place to list medications being used, however.

The purpose of this discussion is to show how the doctor or other family professional may obtain a three-dimensional medical picture, if you will. This picture would provide the physician with a basis for asking further questions when meeting personally with the (new) client. Meetings with doctors vary from about five minutes to ten minutes of interaction. Lab tests and onsite diagnostics might take an additional five to ten minutes. The likelihood is that the waiting room time is easily about ten times longer than the doctor-patient meeting.

These "five minute doctors" are pressured for time and pressured by patients to give them attention. Under these circumstances, it may seem difficult, and perhaps unfair, to expect these practitioners and/ or their staff to involve themselves in more detailed intakes.

Yet consider that doctors don't distribute new questionnaires after the initial office visit. Consider, too, that when a patient approaches the receptionist desk, they are asked only a few questions: "What is your name?" "What seems to be the problem?" and "What is your insurance?"

These are not extraordinary questions; they are basic. But these basic questions are usually followed with, "Please take a seat." There does appear to be some time here for a brief questionnaire that can cover additional, reflective sorts of questions.

It is typically American to treat identified symptoms. Yet how often do individuals become impatient when symptoms recur without any further diagnosis? It is very dangerous to oversimplify and treat symptoms without understanding their cause.

Perhaps the physician wanting to treat a child should work more closely with both parents and school administrators in order to collect enough data to determine the child's needs and effective protocols. It is very important for the medical family professional to determine if mental health interventions, whether individual or family therapy, might be a less costly and more immediate choice of intervention.

Once identified, the child's symptoms can be easily observed by his or her teachers, who would be given instructions for further monitoring. A teacher or administrator may be viewed by a conflicted child as more stable than an arguing parent. The child may find such a school official to be the one most able to offer protection from emotional and/or physical abuse and more reassuring about the future.

It would be prudent for professionals to treat physical changes based on acknowledgement and acceptance of the "root cause." Additionally effective might be a broader, remedial approach or assessment to assist the patient in coping with both the present and recurring condition.

The school where the child spends most of her day may be considered the "first line of defense," or diagnosis. The school might be the first and most immediate place for observing a child's changed behaviors, such as truancy. Once identified, a child may be "targeted" by teachers, administrators, and or health professionals for further monitoring. But only with the permission of the custodial parents may the school administer psychological interventions or meetings with a school social worker.

School guidance counselor Patricia Bird of Tiverton, R.I., explains that teachers may refer children for observation by a special student evaluation team meeting (ETM), which includes a social worker, principal, therapist, and parent.

If a teacher suspects that there is a weak or threatening dynamic in a student's home, the teacher can request that the ETM be established to examine what dynamics are present in the household and, furthermore, to administer evaluation through preliminary but broad-based testing. Though in most school systems parents must give their approval for any invasive investigations such as this, advocates within the school will push through the evaluation process in the guise of federally approved testing for special educational needs.

There are three aspects to this testing: academic, psychological, and social/emotional. Each of these tests complements the other in that the ETM has a mission, "to see if there are significant discrepancies between the norm and individual outcomes."[205] A social history intake is given to a parent by the social worker. A school psychologist administers the psycho/social test to the student, and then compares the child's development and personality levels with the student's academic performance. When it appears that something else seems to be impacting the child's scores, the school authorities can make referrals to psychiatric care if need be. But, stated Bird, "it doesn't take a rocket scientist to see the parallel with the rates of medicated young students and the rates of parental divorce in any community."[206]

Sometimes a conflicted child will perceive another adult as a teacher, guidance counselor, or administrator as more stable and more approachable than an arguing parent. If that person is an FP, then there may be mandatory reporting of abuses or there may be simply a discovery of the child's thoughts and feelings about their home life and changes within it.

But family professionals often admit that they fear discussion with their client about their family's status including marriage stability and challenges. One physician reported that it would compromise his client relationship and open him to the threat of a lawsuit. Therefore, it may be reasonable to consider how a family professional might ethically engage their client in such discussion. This inquiry might help to confirm the perception of a parent's marital difficulties and allow for client referrals to other helpful professionals. Might not an appropriate, routine assessment be constructed to forewarn and prevent a couple's relationship and an individual's mental health from deteriorating? The challenge is to a) legitimize such inquiry and b) empower the professional with approved protocols to identify existing family disturbances, even pathologies. This effort may help adult family members to acknowledge negative or changing dynamics. This effort can help raise a new consciousness within the family. It can help all family members to acknowledge the presence of potentially escalating problems. Through referrals to other community sources, it can assist the family to arrest further progressions and *synergistic family negations*—those factors that inhibit successful problem and conflict resolutions.

Perhaps the physician wanting to treat a child should work more closely with both parents and school administrators in order to collect enough data to determine the child's needs and effective protocols. It is very important for the medical family professional to determine whether mental health interventions, whether individual or family therapy, might be a less costly and more immediate intervention.

The primary aim of this discussion is to encourage the many different community-based professionals to intervene with questions and comprehensive intake procedures, and to provide information and referrals to their client. Professionals who know family members through work, school, physician services, mental health services, church, and other places of interaction may ask client permission to work collaboratively with the client's other professionals. Importantly, if a family professional identified someone dealing with health or procedural issues, then it ought to be a protocol for the FP to ask the client for permission to help. Then, reasonable advice and referrals might help to reduce family vulnerability to parental separation and divorce.

True, there are privacy concerns such as those mandated by HIPAA (Health Insurance Portability and Accountability Act of 1996).[207] This federal law, act 104-191, was introduced to standardize health claims among insurers, to protect the sharing of demographic information, and to additionally provide for medical expense savings accounts. The act also considers what or how a professional's further inquiry might be a breach of one's rights to privacy. As noted above, a physician expressed fear that incorporating questions about a client's marital life might bring repercussions, including malpractice lawsuits. HIPAA may delimit such inquiry or be augmented so as to enable data gathering about sensitive or traumatic domestic matters.

The constraints of privacy and the constraints of professional boundaries are realistic. They need to be addressed responsibly but with the overriding concern that it is for the health of our families and the resiliency of our society that professionals consider working together. As family professionals admit to missed intervention opportunities, then it is likely that they will rally together to discover some acceptable intervention format. Their respective professional associations may become more committed to mapping a protocol for identifying an existing family dysfunction and the formal means for addressing it.

Might a more detailed intake procedure address a timely need for additional, appropriate interventions or professional referrals? Perhaps training those with client intake responsibilities to tactfully ask revealing questions will help identify vulnerable family members. There may be a further acceptable questionnaire design that can identify individual behaviors, family dynamics, spousal interactions, parenting quality, and work stress. Just a few questions may elicit answers leading to an improved quality of life for the patient client or deter them from serious personal harm in the short term.

Once questions are answered, then the next protocol is to determine what staff need to do with the answers to questions like, "How are you today? What's new? What's happening in your life? You look tired—Why?" Answers to such questions might in fact be welcomed by the client/patient/customer/parent who had been unable to articulate the feelings circulating through his mind, gut, and heart. Such questions will certainly validate feelings and self-perceptions and restore self-esteem should it be diminished or lost.

Knowing the questions to ask is based on experience and education. Education of both the parents and the professionals is the foundation of appropriate intervention.

Parent Education

In some thirty states, family courts require that the "best interests of the child" be conveyed through a required course for parents seeking divorce, custody, or access agreements. These courses, termed "parent education," are usually six hours long and consist of lecture, film, and Q&A. The courses are focused on the best interests of children and what parents need to know about child development and communication skills.

A fundamental concept referenced in family court rulings is the children's best interests statute discussed earlier. Invariably, the use of this statute is very confusing, open to many interpretations, and a cause for continuing litigation, post-divorce. Consider Connecticut's best interests statute (46b-56), which reads as follows:

> "In making or modifying any order with respect to custody or visitation, the court shall: be guided by the best interest of the child, giving consideration to the wishes of the child if the child is of sufficient age and capable of forming an intelligent preference, provided in making the initial order the court may take into consideration the causes for dissolution of the marriage or legal separation if such causes are relevant in a determination of the best interest of the child and consider whether the party satisfactorily completed participation in a parenting education class established pursuant to section 46b-69b."[208]

This best interests statute was updated in 2005 to reflect the seven-year-old requirement that separated parents complete a six-hour parent education program. Connecticut's Best Interests of The Child Standard referenced above presents a dilemma in litigation. It provides no specific benchmarks to help determine what may constitute differentiation of beneficial, damaging, or benign parenting qualities. Neither does the statute offer any reasonable criterion for parenting ability, short of the mandated six-hour parenting course, before court-ordered custody decisions are made.

Within the statute, there is no mention of the salient components of the parent education program. Indeed, there is no discussion within the statute, however updated, to reflect developmental abilities of the children to make their own decisions. There is no specificity about *causes* for marital or legal separation. Clearly, much is left to interpretation, in spite of the plethora of sociological and psychological research that has emerged in the last fifteen years.

Parent education programs can become much more effective if curricula provide psychosocial education about families in which parents are disengaging. There should be a clear acknowledgement of who is to be included in a family diagram. There may have been mom and dad living at home with the children. But do families also include grandparents, cousins, aunts, and uncles? What can be said of neighborhoods and communities? Friends? Parent education frequently overlooks these relationships, just as the courts do not take into account their importance.

What might an order that a parent enroll in a parent education class do for that parent's self-esteem? If one has parented through the toddler and preadolescent years, then, does the court order suggest that that parent has parenting deficiencies? Is the court saying that there is mistrust about one's parenting abilities? Consider that these parents needed no court orders for parenting classes when raising their children prior to the current litigation. Additionally, consider the timing of these court orders. The courses are required during what may be called "the heat of the moment." Parents required to take these classes are doing so at the order of the court, at a time when emotions are at their peak, when anger, disappointment, and fear are greatest.

Can we expect most parents to sit through a course that is instructive and court ordered without feeling defensive and personally violated? Are these parents capable of absorbing instructive information at a time of depression and animosity? Indeed, if asked, would any parent agree that someone else knows what is best for his or her children? The likely answer to any of these questions is no, especially when that someone else is the state.

Though there is little study of and formal evaluation of the worth of parent education courses, it is not hard to accept that a cookie cutter approach to any education effort will just not work for all "students." If children mirror or respond to parents' emotional and behavioral states, then perhaps parent education should be more focused on the parent. That some twenty-five percent of separated, divorced parents are products of highly conflicted relationships suggests that a cookie cutter approach to educating parents will not necessarily work. This is so when these relationships are exacerbated by pre- and post-custody and child access court hearings.[209]

A parent educator, I have found state mandated co-parenting curricula which focus nearly exclusively on the needs of children, and to the detriment of the parents' individual emotional and psychological journeys. Courses are pedantic, instructing parents as to what to think, how to behave, and explain how their choices will impact their co-parenting. Courses ignore the plight of the single and separated parent, the parent now thrust into divorce and all the many fears and traumas that may accompany the process.

I have advocated that courses be created to reflect the new emotional journey of the parent, to acknowledge their new circumstances and financial and social changes which course through their mind and heart.

The nature of co-parenting courses today are increasingly required to show research based outcomes. This is a difficult process I would argue since courses are required by states mandating these courses to be taken within the first thirty days of divorce or child custody court motions.

I collaborated with Connecticut psychotherapists Lori Carpenos and forensic psychologist Nellie Fillipopoulos, PsyD, to produce an alternative parent education curriculum for divorcing parents in the state of Connecticut. The collaboration produced a unique curriculum that acknowledges a parent's emotional transitions following the disturbance when love ends and separation or divorce ensues. Our goal was to become more parent-centered as opposed to child-centered since, as I had referenced Menninger earlier, "what's done to children at home, they will do to society." A parent-focused program may produce better outcomes through increased communication options for parents, reduced hostility between parents, and therefore improved child behaviors, attitudes, self-esteem, and comfort. If indeed children mirror their parents, then should not the parents be assisted concurrently with the children?

Parent education should be amended to resolve such questions as, "How is it possible for separated parents, often from different social, ethnic, and racial backgrounds, to prepare for the continued sharing of child rearing and custody arrangements?"

We recommend educating parents through their own cultural eyes and ears using language and values that they can understand— teaching parents about their children's reactions to parental splits, but also, importantly, how parents may improve their own relationship so that parental separation may be temporary and not result in a divorce—or murder, or suicide. Some heinous domestic crimes have been committed by a spouse frustrated by the inability to reasonably cope with family dysfunction. A vigilant professional can intervene.

How might a parent's life experience affect one's ability to understand the needs of their children and one's ability to effectively co-parent? How can the courts and school systems as primary social educators address an individual's cross-cultural beliefs, values, and expectations?

Over thirty states provide some form of parent education, a four- to six-hour program for divorcing parents. This program is a requirement, with its central piece examining how parental hostilities are not in the "best interests of children." I heard proclaimed in a parent education meeting that "99 percent of parents think the course is terrific."[210] But, I'd argue, statistics on parent satisfaction were unreliable since parents were more relieved to complete their course requirement than they were with the learning. Few statistics be found on parent/student satisfaction in any other state to date.

One may reasonably question if many, or any, parents think attending a course on how to parent is "terrific." When each parent blames the other for their marital breakdown, how can these spurned lovers find solace and help in a four to six-hour, court-ordered and state mandated co-parenting class which focuses exclusively on the children? A program of just four to six hours, whether in one sitting or spread over several classroom meetings is no panacea for most parents who are suffering great emotional and financial pain. Online courses are equally deficient.

Though few in number nationally, child kidnapping and murder-suicides are symptomatic of incomplete or inappropriate court decisions. Public school students who murder peers and teachers may be additional symptoms of problematic parental divorce and separation. It is urgent that parents be helped to recognize their own emotional changes and to be helped in coping with them. A depressed parent, foundering in front of the television when "visiting" with his children is not a great model for the children. The children won't doubt their love for that parent, but they will doubt the parent's ability to parent them.

Children thrive when parents provide appropriate guidance. Children need age appropriate leadership, including discipline, love, and nurturing. A parent who labors against his or her own helplessness and woe is incapable of adequate parenting, at least during this troubled period.

If the courts are first to be approached when a marriage collapses, then shouldn't the courts offer information, education, and support for families so that they can "go forward" in their lives? Current parent curricula will be better received when parents are acknowledged for their current status, when they are validated for their emotional straights, and can be assured that there will light at the end of the tunnel, somehow, in some period of time. Essentially, co-parenting courses can and should include elements of emotional support. This can be done when there is such aforementioned validation, and personal discussion.

But, I would also recommend that co-parenting courses be offered parents more than once during their child custody and or divorce litigation. When stressed and emotionally charged, one cannot pay attention. However as time and distance pass from the trauma of separation and divorce, one is more settled, and better prepared to receive guidance and instruction. They can feel more confident in taking action steps, and allow themselves new approaches necessary for satisfactory shared parenting and emotionally safe communications with children and former spouse.

Both parents who love their children need to be supported in their quest to maintain loving relationships with their children after separation and divorce. As courts become more conscious of both parents' desire to remain involved in the raising of their children post-separation and divorce, they may accept new procedures for reducing conflict among the parents and cease being a battleground for resolving conflict. They will then become a more revered symbol of justice. Education through professional development may prove a significant means for change.

Professional Development

With relevant education, FP's will be more aware of their capacity to offer more effective assistance to families. Professional Development though not new is required for professional license renewals and thus would be an important catalyst for new learning into their client interactions. As an example, medical professionals so educated with greater understandings of family transitions may be more rapidly identify those patients who may be both physically and emotionally vulnerable. Therefore, they can help nullify the harmful effects on children who are victimized as a consequence of their parents' separation and divorce.

Licensed professionals as therapists, attorneys, mediators, health care providers, all promise to abide by the covenants of their respective occupations—perhaps to advocate until their client should win through litigation, or to medically intervene when patients are ill, or to treat a client's emotional issues with respect and dignity, or to provide spiritual counsel to those seeking help with marriage and family concerns.

Individually, the family professional can provide instruction, reference material, referrals, and reassurances. Through more sensitive and complete questioning can validate client's pain, clarify the problems extant in the marital or cohabitation home, and validate a client's right to question their feelings and responses to fragmenting family relationships.

Adapting a more detailed intake as a routine protocol will no doubt help elevate clients' spirits and sense of self-worth. It may prevent a conflict that could have led to murder or suicide. Matters relating to divorce, child access, and child custody are yet, in the main, litigated, and whereas these matters affect all family and extended family members, professional collaborations become increasingly helpful in mitigating destructive outcomes.

Professional education that addresses parent separation, divorce, child custody, parenting, and child development will empower all community change agents and family professionals with the skills needed for successful interventions. Valuable sources for professionals requiring continuing education units as CEUs, CLE's, CME's and professional training include the professional associations across the professional social service spectrum including Boards of Education, Bar Associations, and other professional associations such as the American Psychological Association, National Association of Social Workers, and the American Medical Association.

As families journeying through separation and divorce may are prone to emotional conflict, I suggest it vital for each profession to learn of the changed and challenging family dynamics. One way to mitigate the damages associated with litigation, parental alienation, and associated child and parent outcomes may be through continuing education of all family professionals who work with family members. I would suggest too that in each profession's education be curriculum taught by a specialist from each significant discipline as mentioned above lecture about their specialty and discuss the complementary goals when working with families. Attorneys who advocate, psychologists who examine and testify, and judges who give temporary and final orders are those family professionals. Required continuing education may be the key to providing them with professional development.

Continued education of court and other family professionals through formal, concentrated training curricula may yet be the most effective means to ensure an equitable flow of family law decisions. One form of this training may be carried out through a resource person known as a "counselor educator." Quoting Maples, "The role of the counselor educator is uniquely appropriate to meet the needs of judges. The counselor educator is trained in the areas of interpersonal communications, including nonverbal communication; confronting personal values and attitudes as they impact on professional decision-making; facilitating clients' abilities to express themselves; and encouraging reluctant clients, family systems and stages and tasks in human development. *These are specific skills, techniques and areas of knowledge that are overlooked in law school.*"[211]

Graduate and other professional training programs are providing knowledge useful for those who wish to become effective primary and secondary family professionals. Those institutions that train human service professionals are increasingly valuable change agents. University departments of human development, education, family studies, and developmental psychology may also act as change agents, particularly if appropriate courses in marriage, family, human communication, and contemporary sociology are required.

The educated FP and FPT will most effectively assist parents to mitigate their pain and frustrations caused by separation, divorce, and court litigation of custody and visitation issues. These issues add to a parent's frustrations but may be reduced when the FP can get in touch with the primary components of the parents' personal life—the "life spheres" mentioned above. Furthermore, a curriculum of integrated learning could be designed by a panel of specialists from across disciplines. Such a curriculum might impart trans-disciplinary information that is conducive to professional collaboration. I envision a curriculum based on lectures and workshops that can be presented at an interdisciplinary conference on improving outcomes for children.

This curriculum could be administered around the country, with built-in flexibility for adapting to the needs and attitudes unique to each geographic region. The curriculum would provide continuing education credits applicable to a range of disciplines, as well as universally relevant psychosocial understandings. To reach different populations, representatives of each population would conduct the course.

If one assumes that more effective service delivery can reduce the impact of family dysfunction, then those providing the services must receive the best possible training. Family professionals who directly influence the lives and decisions of family leaders and family members should:

1. acknowledge weakening bonds among family members;
2. understand the challenges within a changing family structure;
3. identify those challenges; and
4. offer treatment either through their intervention or through referral.

As the first line of defense, these professionals are most immediately able to observe, diagnose, and treat family members. With a trained eye, they can identify household dynamics that indicate conflict and also refer individual parents and children to other professional services before, during, and following marital/partner conflict.

Improved individual family member outcomes can be associated with more effective interdisciplinary interventions. Professionals may become better equipped when current family professionals and students in professional schools acquire new learning.

One challenge is to incorporate new learning in pre-professional education. The other challenge is to identify the structures (methodology and framework) that enable professionals to learn, through vocational training, continuing education, and other professional contexts. With respect to continuing education, it must be understood that professional practices are busy with reports and professional compliance procedures as added tasks outside the one on one client interaction. There, new learning for the professional must be delivered in a convenient manner, whether through classroom, public lecture or web-based learning. A necessary goal of this new learning must be that understanding potential family member outcomes be the primary, urgent part of their client focus.

Without professional education, few opportunities will appear for alternative resolutions of critical family issues. None of these opportunities will have any great measurable effect unless professionals working with families learn how their role can be more successfully utilized in assisting these families through collaborations with other family professionals in creating a synergistic healing modality, unique for their region and their family court. Additionally, professional development from across disciplines will be most successful when

FPs commits to the learning process, and their respective professional associations endorse it.

A Case for New Court Services

Upon reviewing their data collected throughout the longest study of children post-divorce, Wallerstein, Lewis, and Blakeslee concluded, "If we want to improve our divorce culture, we can begin with better services for families that are breaking up."[212]

An immediate service to litigants is changing the courthouse environment so that parents can sit in chairs or couches, have access to private discussion areas or conference rooms, and then enter the courtroom when their case is to be heard. Rather than standing in a public area, hearing discussion of their case before others while anxiously awaiting their own hearings, family members' privacy could be respected.

The courts might also help parents understand the logical processes of the presiding justices and their court orders. This would take the form of a debriefing where the litigants, together or individually, are given an explanation of the meaning of the issued court orders and their significance, as well as options now available.

The debriefing would be delivered with empathy and with acknowledgement of possible disappointment and confusion. Outside the highly pressured courtroom, a litigant would find a supportive environment and an individual who cares about his/her situation.

A detailed debriefing could provide referrals to other agencies and even generate protocols for healthy living including diet and exercise. The individuals who choose healthier behaviors will then likely solidify their predisposition for improved care. This should lead to additional, positive life choices. This will also lead to better role modeling for children, which is essential for their mental health.

As family service caseworkers generally administer matters before the court hearing, they might also provide an even more valuable function by helping the couple resolve the child access issues before departing the courthouse. The caseworkers could in this way prevent further tragedies.

NEW COURT PARADIGMS: A CASE FOR CHANGE

If the courts could enforce decisions for shared parenting and joint custody as easily as for child support, there would be less need for child support enforcement services and fewer incidences of outrage in the form of child kidnapping, abuse, and domestic violence.

Fewer cases would reduce family court expenses. It would alleviate the daily pressure on judges and attorneys and perhaps allow for more efficient scheduling of cases by type of motions.

Movement away from the litigation battlefield of winners and losers towards collaborative law and mediation are increasingly more viable alternatives to narrowing the chasms of custody and child access. Mediation has proven to be one significant approach to lessoning the conflict between litigants. Conflict is reduced, financial expenditures are lessened, and both children and parents are less stressed by the family reformation process that separation and divorce compel. More amiable resolution of conflicts also results in more child access time and more timely payment of court-ordered child support. But mediation works best when all parties agree to the process or in those states that mandate mediation prior to court appearances for hearings and final orders.

There will be change in the courtroom when there is an acknowledgement of emotional losses to the children and a belief that the court must mitigate those losses. It may be expected that when family law courts recognize that they have the power to enforce compliance with existing orders, say, for child access, the courts will then have exercised their duty to help all family members.

A Case for a Unified Courtroom

In Dade County, Florida, a unified court design enables an expeditious use of the judicial system in adjudicating, enforcing, sentencing, treating, and educating in matters of domestic violence.[213] The goal of the Dade County Domestic Violence Court (DCDVC) is to "reduce family violence" through the use of an interdisciplinary team. This innovative effort includes intensive victim services and seeks not only punishment, but also treatment for abusers.

Dade County courts acknowledge that violent homes present great hardships and threaten children, so parent education is essential. Judges are specifically trained for the mission of the court and its potential for offering interventions.

The other unique paradigm is that judges in Dade County stay with their individual cases from start to finish. Such consistency allows for continued objectivity in case management, less time required for hearings, and swifter decisions. Caseloads are reduced, pressure on "the bench" is lessoned, and family members feel acknowledged.

In Connecticut, when I served on the Governor's Commission on Divorce, Custody, and Children, it was found that a frequent complaint from divorcing parents was that judges never remained with a case.[214] As superior court judges are frequently reassigned—normally every two years—a family court proceeding will have two or more judges during the litigation process, which lasts a year or more. Judges who are new to ongoing cases must learn the nuances, the pending arguments, and the positions of the litigating parties. The judge requires additional time to become familiar with each case as litigants continue to reargue motions pending from earlier appearances.

The change of judges can be especially burdensome for parents and children who often labor through months of unwanted or emotionally difficult child and family therapy and postponement of hearings—a strategy used by opposing attorneys to weaken the other side. Child custody and child access decisions generally depend upon psychological evaluations and other therapeutic work which, upon one court order, won't be completed in a timely fashion or need to be understood by a judge new to that court's bench. Thus, child access is frequently delayed while these processes ensue and hearings are postponed. Most courts permit this, though it is cumbersome and unfair to all parties.

NEW PARADIGMS FOR VISITATION

The Rhode Island Department of Children, Youth, and Family (DCYF) underwrites a unique supervised visitation program provided by Families Together. Families Together is an important therapeutic and diagnostic resource, primarily for reunification of children in the foster care system with their biological parents.

While Rhode Island's DCYF provides such services as counseling, parenting classes, and foster care, Families Together was among the first providers I had known which sees the entire family interact for extended periods of time, thus providing a more complete picture of the family. Caseworkers rely on the objective viewpoint of the therapists to design a permanency plan for the child, which is required under the Adoption and Safe Families Act. What also distinguishes this program is its location at the Providence Children's Museum, a neutral site in that there are no courtrooms, no attorney offices, and no segregated areas for parent-child interaction.

In Connecticut, the Southern Connecticut State University Family Therapy Clinic joined with the New Haven Family Alliance in a unique collaboration to encourage poor, minority fathers to become involved in the lives of their children. The alliance sought to provide remedial services directly to its client population. The university wanted to increase the client population using its services.

Guidelines issued by the alliance state that "routine visitation is appropriate for families in which each of the biological parents is able to work reasonably and appropriately, albeit separately, with the children. Parents in conflict, however, "are often unable to negotiate with each other regarding planning for visits, have difficulty keeping their behavior towards each other within appropriate bounds when they are in direct contact, and are unable to adhere to plans or court orders."[215]

The two programs above reflect differing purposes for mediating parent and child relationships through supervised sessions: first, for reunification between children, often separated in the temporary foster care system where the state is temporary guardian. The second is where parental conflict is considered to be a predominant inhibitor to normal parent and child interactions, thus requiring a neutral location for the noncustodial parent and child to meet.

Each of the programs reflects the usual mission for supervised access. The mission is to observe, guide, support, and strengthen and normalize the parent-child relationship. The Southern Connecticut State University Family Clinic guidelines state that "the program is intended as a temporary measure to create some 'protected' time during which parents work on improving the parental environment for the child and sharing a responsibility to work toward developing more appropriate ways of being with each other so that children are able to reap the benefits derived from cooperative parents."[216]

On its face, the goal for supervised visitation seems protective, encouraging, and significant. But when an observer visits the facility, they will find that the parent-child interaction takes place in a single room of approximately ten feet by fifteen feet. The visitation is monitored by a third party physically present throughout the session or with the third party observing the interaction through a one-way mirror.

Comparing the two programs, the first relates to the goal of changing the child-parent relationship from one of foster care to reunification with shared home. The second relates to the goal of providing some common area where children and parents can improve their relationship without the overriding mission of long-term placement. Both programs involve protecting the child through careful monitoring of emotional intimacy, nurturing, and dependency by trained staff. Both realize that child access for both parents is in the child's best interest. Yet both see child access as having different outcomes. The first quote relates to a clinical process that takes place in a stimulating children's museum. The second quote relates to a clinical process that takes place in a sterile, uncomfortable, single room.

There are many mixed messages here. When clinical, supervised visitation takes place, it does so with the first premise that a parent is a danger and needs supervision. This supervision provides little or no opportunity for the parent and child to be comfortable and to engage in activity that may stimulate and aid conversation, care, and nurturing.

Those professionals who provide supervised access/visitation admit to using facilities that are great for clinical observation, but that may be poor for aiding parent-child relationships. Said O'Donnell, "Meeting the challenges of parenthood through effective communication and nurturing behavior does change the dynamic in their relations with their children. A supportive learning environment for family visitation helps parents develop a sense of their own competence and gain skills in caring for and managing their children."[217]

The Families Together program is changing DCYF practice by helping social workers to better understand and engage in experiential learning with parents during visitation. At least two days a week a staff member is available in each of DCYF's four regional offices to assist with visits and offer guidance to social workers and families. In addition, Families Together staff works with DCYF's Child Welfare Training Institute to provide formal training in experiential learning and family-centered practice.

Families Together helps social workers move from passively observing to actively helping parents to understand their own roles and responsibilities in meeting the needs of their children. Families Together does not provide a standard parenting course; rather it presents opportunities for parents to find their own solution to situations and circumstances involving their children that they felt they could not handle before. It gives them hands-on experience and immediate feedback as they master parenting skills. Often parents need to have a better sense of their own importance in the lives of their children.

Locations that are neutral, that provide nonresidential parents and their children a non-threatening meeting place are valuable for parents deemed by the court as needing supervised sessions. These court decisions are sometimes determined by fear allegations, recommendations by evaluating therapists, and when the court sees no alternatives, given a great time span (usually in months) since the last parent-child interaction. Sometimes, the courts are unsure if a parent may pose through threat to possible kidnapping or violence.

It is important to understand some of the factors that concern researchers and social theorists so that courts might be educated to implement more efficient and more compassionate decisions for children. Based on correlation of outcomes to present policy, family law, and litigation procedures, it should behoove such gatekeepers as family court judges to themselves advocate for changes in court services and community resources.

The court generally has no idea of a couple's plight until their litigation begins. Most litigating couples do not appear earlier because of family abuse, criminal allegations, or other matters. "Essentially, for most families, there is no 'prior' history; the court has no idea about the quality of the marriage before the motions for divorce are initially heard. The court has no preconceived notion about the individuals then appearing together for custody or child access."[218]

Yet outcomes of most domestic cases are the same because the fundamental legal tenets are the same. Court rulings are based on interpretations of "children's best interests" rather than some measure of joint custody or shared parenting. These decisions redefine each parent's capacity for raising their children.

I am reminded of two tragic cases some years ago in Connecticut. As I recall reading and frequently mention in presentations, there were several courts miles apart which did not heed the psychological indicators present during the initial litigation. Rather, they took a cookie cutter approach to legal decision-making.

One court ordered both parents home to design their own

custody agreement and return to court with it completed. Instead of returning with the agreement, the result was the attempted murder of the couple's toddler and the murder suicide of the parents.

Two months later, in another court jurisdiction, a mother kidnapped the child from her scheduled visitation session and fled to Pennsylvania. This happened in spite of the custodial father's earlier warning to the court of the mother's stated intentions to kidnap the child.

These are cases which reflect too often the extremes of child access litigation and results from court decisions.

Child access has many components that factor in to the quality of developmentally appropriate child outcomes. Some children are treated too much like adults for their age; some try to fill a leadership vacuum when a parent leaves the marital home. Some children regress when visiting with an absent parent, seeking the love and attention they had wanted for weeks, months, or longer.

Research increasingly demonstrates the relationship court orders have on parent-child relationships. It is important, though, that rights to access be more specifically detailed in family law statutes, particularly in contentious custody litigation. It may be that new state statutes that allow the holding of the alienating parent accountable may deter further contentious custody litigation. Such statute changes might dictate acceptable punishments for those who hold their children's emotions hostage through alienation. Till then, individual parents suffering the loss of contact with their children will need incredible coping skills. A coordinated, interdisciplinary approach to these people will help them contain their anger, control their depression, and eliminate their hopelessness. The absence of such interventions gives reason for inappropriate and even extreme behaviors of alienation (emotional kidnapping), abduction, and violence.

The litigation process can be improved by implementing the recommendations of the American Bar Association, and current research on mediated agreements will limit hostile litigations that seek more control, punishment, and vilification. New standards from intake to referral may improve parent and child outcomes following custody, child access, and related divorce actions. Then, the focus can be on children's needs for their parents' love. A Leo Buscaglia poem beautifully describes a child's emotional needs:

"But I am told that love is stronger than walls,
and in this, lies my only hope.
So beat down those walls with your firm but gentle hands,
for the child within me is very sensitive and can't grow behind walls.
So don't give up, I need you." [219]

What might be a parental imperative for raising children? In other words, what fundamental bit of knowledge can we offer our children? Says Buscaglia, "Not only do they (children) have this incredible uniqueness, but they also have something that sometimes we forget about. They are also potentiality. They are much more undiscovered than they are discovered. And there's the wonder of it. It doesn't matter where they are; they're only just beginning and the big magical trip of life is digging it all out and discovering the wonderful you."[220]

We need context when raising children. Ernst Haeckel's contested biological theory that ontogeny recapitulates phylogeny affected the beliefs about children's developmental needs.[221] Haeckel tried to show that successive generations grow to emulate prior generational forms. But successive generations do adapt to environmental changes. Life begets life; all life is driven by survival of the species through replication and reproduction. That it takes two people to make a child means that there is a sharing of responsibility in that creation; there is a sharing of responsibility that should continue in the raising of children from that union. Humans are given the ability to think, to make choices. These choices are dictated by cultural values and an individual's perceptions, during different developmental stages, of what behaviors and attitudes are correct. Parents come in many colors, from many countries, with different faiths, speaking different languages; hence, the cultural diversity within our species.

Parents, too, have different physical attributes and abilities, mental health issues, family histories, differing educational records, and different communication skills and lifestyles. The greatest common thread among parents is that they have children. All children, too, have a common thread: children have implicit trust that their parents will provide for their needs, including security, food, clothing, and shelter. They also have the equally important need for emotional support and guidance.

It is the parent's universal role to provide physical protection and nurturing for their children. Parents also reward and punish children's behaviors based on the parent's ranking of acceptable behaviors, which is also based on their own emotional responses to different stimuli. The need for parents is postulated by clinicians and demonstrated by government statistics, many of which have been cited numerous times in this document.

"What's done to children, they will do to society," was psychiatrist Karl Menninger's pronouncement more than fifty years ago.[222] That parents are models for children is clear when we see how hatred and bigotry, political affiliation, culinary preferences, and domestic abuse are passed on from one generation to the next. How society views certain attitudes and behaviors is reinforced by the parents, families, and neighborhoods that our children grow up within. Yet, again, one's family and life experience may not be acceptable to society's social and legal systems.

In most systems such as courts, schools, and the workplace, there is a concerted effort at social homogeneity or uniformity. Except for language translations, there are few diversity programs that are formalized and that recognize the multitude of cultural values present in this nation. The legal and educational systems in particular acknowledge cultural differences through language translations. More formal recognition may be through show and tell demonstrations. These systems may deal more successfully with diversity issues by acknowledging cultural differences, communicating through cultural ambassadors as was suggested earlier in the paper, and using focus groups to share understandings of cultural priorities and adaptations with respect to parenting styles, beliefs, practices, and values. (Can you imagine family courts using community-based focus groups to create dialogue and mutual understanding?)

Former federal child support enforcement commissioner Judge David Gray Ross stated that "child support is more than financial, it is also emotional."[223] Child access needs to be discussed in the same breath as financial child support because both are legal rights of the child pending parent separation, divorce, and custody assignment. It is argued that the child's right to parent access is protected by the constitution. This is suggested in many state statutes relating to the child's best interests doctrine. However, few courts remove a child from one parent's domicile if they do not comply with visitation. They also easily order visitation, reduce shared parenting time, and do not consider the child's desires for extended family access. Reasons for that behavior varies, and requires more investigation.

VIRTUAL FAMILIES, VISUAL REALITIES: WHAT CHILDREN SEE

As Karl Menninger pointed out, parents do model behaviors and communication styles for their children. Adults should not underestimate the effect of overheard telephone conversations, responses to slow turnpike drivers (who just happen to be directly in front of us or in the left-hand passing lane), missed deadlines, mother-in-law visits, overcooked home dinners, or an employer's request for overtime—just some examples which have elicited differing responses in many homes.

What do children see in their home? What is it that children learn there? Perhaps one should reflect on what children are expected to learn in school compared to what they are expected to learn at home, given the limited time that two overworked and tired parents can provide. Think of the No Child Left Behind Act of 2001. Why is it that schools are assigned with the increased responsibility, if not, sole responsibility for educating our children?

It seems that "no child left behind" is essentially a parenting goal;

parents seek to strengthen the ability of their children to survive in an increasingly sophisticated, competitive environment. We have seen that there are threats from external terrors, implicit in the fears that we have for our own society's safety as America has embarked on a path towards preemptive security measures. The external political pressures may combine with the continuing internal financial pressures upon families to weaken already fragile relationships between spouses and partners. As the education system has taken on its assignments to educate our children, it has taken upon itself a value system imposed and governed by national doctrines, not taking into account differing cultural identities.

So, what are parents to do? Many have given up. During three years of interviews and discussions on New England college campuses, I found that approximately half of the freshman and sophomores reported that it was their parents who first discussed the mechanics of sex with them when they were between the ages of ten and twelve. Beyond that, parents avoided the subjects of romance, sexual relationships, and communication between adolescents and young adults. It appears that parents have allowed middle school and high school health classes to handle these critical topics. Yet, because of federal funding constraints, these classes tend to focus primarily on sexual abstinence and the distribution of condoms. In other words, parents have appointed our school systems as de facto resources for training our young to engage in behaviors deemed responsible for those who are the sexually active.

Is puberty and sex the primary indicator of adult needs? Many teens think so. When do we teach our youth about responsibility that needs to be associated with communication? Working parents have little time to spend educating their children about values or how to make moral decisions. Are children in a labyrinth of social confusion during the middle school and high school years? Some point to schools like Columbine as evidence of this being so. In the college years, young adults enter the roller coasters of emotional experience and overconfidence in idea formation and acceptance. Schools are frequently unable to adequately assess students emotionally and psychologically unless both parents agree to some perhaps intrusive assistance by school social workers and school psychologists.

It may therefore be incumbent upon school administrations to assess whether campuses offer sufficient resources to address the numerous confusions centered on both body and mind.

HELPING FAMILIES HEAL: IDENTIFYING FAMILY NEEDS

Knowing the reasons why parents separate or divorce may help in preserving relationships. Marriage counselors, therapists, clergy, and even attorneys might offer effective interventions when marriages are troubled. Premarital counseling might become more helpful in saving relationships by offering strategies for managing stress, anger, and disappointment within the marriage.

Sociologists seek to identify population patterns and pattern changes. Observing change is part of their purpose. The other part is to look for correlation in population behaviors, point out causes and effects of observed behavior, and then explain how the behavior might help strengthen or weaken the community. Aberrant behavior may be viewed as negative behavior that contributes to other social ills or perhaps as a natural tendency for a society to seek balance in its (localized) evolution. Each social scientist is guilty of some subjectivity in drawing conclusions since each is a product of his own society, his own cultural norms, and his own belief systems including psychosocial interpretations based on his own unique family experiences. Such subjectivity is inevitable in nearly every public policy initiative no matter how seemingly beneficial to populations at large.

FAMILY ADAPTATION

It is clear that changed family incomes can have positive or negative effects on the quality of life. As lifestyles do change following parental splits, new routines may emerge.

In *Your Divorce Advisor* by Pruett and Mercer, the authors speak of creating "new family traditions in place of old ones from the divorced family."[224] They speak of including people, values, and a specified day when these new family traditions can be observed.

New family traditions may be pragmatic in the exceptional cases where the noncustodial parent is voluntarily absent from the home. The process of redefining family traditions when those traditions were a nurturing and familiar part of life prior to the family breakdown may cause the children great stress. The new traditions do not account for the experiences and learned values acquired earlier. Neither do they acknowledge what was family tradition, but instead, reinvent or replace the familiar.

Some estranged parents manage to gather together on formerly observed holidays so that their young children still have a sense of consistency. To create new family traditions is an attempt to create a new history and may ultimately prove an unconscious or conscious attempt to negate the love and joys of former holiday and family observances.

Changed and new routines will emerge when a parent departs the child's household and their contact is minimized through court orders and parent agreements. It can also be expected that new companions, remarriages, and blended family conditions will compound the challenges of adaptation.

A New Vocabulary

As professional journals continue to discuss families, divorce, parental separations, and children's best interests, professionals will become more aware of family transformations and permutations. This book is intended to put into perspective the multitude of challenges faced by numerous families today and to help voice the realities that occur when parents choose to separate. The ultimate goal is to mitigate the effects of parental separation and divorce.

Readers are already familiar with family court terminology and the issues that families argue there. Professionals who work with families of divorce also need a common vocabulary that is positive, goal oriented, and proactive. Using these words will help family professionals keep their focus on common goals of

- identifying families where spousal love is failing,
- helping family members cope with the emotional losses that accompany parental breakups,
- maintaining a new dynamic or balance among family members, and
- assisting family members in finding new ways to maintain communication.

I would like to introduce some useful words which will follow:

Healing—"an art of nurturing, teaching the client to open the door to receive a balancing of the mind, body and emotions."[225]

Divorce reconciliation—the process accompanying parental separations wherein they consciously elevate the best interests of their children through acceptance of family change, and continuing love, nurturing, guidance, and emotional and financial support.

Chattel weaponry—those children who are used to punish by restricting shared parenting time, or have been brainwashed or otherwise alienated by one parent, usually the residential parent, against the absent or nonresidential parent.

Hope—"Hope is without tomorrow and sadness is without yesterday." From Harry Remde, artist and physicist, in his essay "Sadness in Art."[226]

Without hope, one's life cannot continue towards increased sustenance, satisfaction, and growth (personal, professional, and artistic). I remember one grandfather's advice: "Don't look backwards because life doesn't go that way."[227]

Joy Berger defines as core the four integral components of healthy treatment that guide music and dance therapists and other holistic practitioners.[228] These four components constitute her core values care, ownership, respect, and empowerment.

Care—base decisions on one's inner core—over and above one's own tastes; "hear, affirm and use (music) from the cultural, religious, and meaning-based 'core' of the person involved."[229] Provide an emotionally safe environment. Allow yourselves to be human with each other.

Ownership—now, affirm and cherish your own music as being uniquely yours. Hear meanings and values it holds for you. Likewise, honor the music of another's life-story, their culture, religion, experiences, and meanings. Honor and affirm these experiences as his/her own, not yours. Let yourself learn from another in the midst of your different life experiences.

Respect— Respect another's emotional boundaries and timetable. Emotional defenses, denial, and resistance foment argument. In the words of Paul McCartney, "Let it be." Especially in your leadership role, respect others' privacy. Respect the larger, universal, spiritual realm.

Empowerment—Seek power and courage for what you can do, surrender and serenity for what is beyond your control. With persons experiencing loss, ask not only, "What do you need?" but also, "What do you not need?" Seek truths, not mere sentimentality. Be responsible, sensitive, and accountable. Tune in to emotional wellness and health, not pathology of pity. Know your power and your powerlessness. Refill, restore, and renew your own energies within—mentally and spiritually.

These words are not peculiar to any new or adjunct vocation. Rather, these words represent a new cultural approval of treating families at risk of divorce and separation. This writer prefers "own" to ownership since each vocabulary word is an action word. Life is action; without action there is no progress and, thus, little satisfaction.

CHAPTER 6

―――∽∾∽―――

FUTURE NEEDS, PRESENT OPPORTUNITIES

WHAT WE KNOW

In 1996, then-first lady Hillary Clinton borrowed an African expression: "We are a village."[230] If courts intrude into the lives of parents and children when parents choose to separate, then why should other societal structures not be used to identify and strengthen such troubled individuals? Of course, more research is needed to examine outcomes for children of parent separations and divorce. On the basis of more-comprehensive data showing how family structures influence child outcomes, public policies could be designed to help preserve parent and child bonds when parents choose to separate.

If behavior, socialization, and academic achievement relate to family structure and dynamics, perhaps school social workers and school psychologists should be empowered to more fully support children. Assessments and investigation of children's behavior, along with non pharmaceutical interventions, might be utilized to mitigate the mirrored effects of a troubled home life. Boards of education and state licensing might also allow administrators, faculty, and specialists to correlate academic achievement with mental health.

The role of schools is especially important since schools are where children spend most of their day. To more effectively use public schools in the manner described above would be a major paradigm shift whose time may have come.

The social agencies within any given state or municipality need to identify where ethnic, cultural, or national immigrant communities exist. It is important to know who the political, economic, religious and/or educational leaders are so that some immediate support system can be readily established for a family in crisis. Identifying these influential leaders or community stakeholders will bring a family out of its isolation and helplessness to meet the community systems at large that need to judge and direct family change as seen in family, juvenile, and probate courts.

Community outreach is a vital, contemporary method to advocate for change. Yet it is important to reflect that the effectiveness of outreach is inversely proportional to the level of shared language competency between message carrier and receiver. It is important that the communication methods and individuals so communicating (male or female, youth or elder, etc.) also be appropriate for and available to the culture.

Professional development and continuing education have mighty roles in providing these prescriptive studies for the legal profession. Professional education both from within the professional school curriculum and through continuing education requirements may enable more effective family interventions. Course discussions in psychology, marriage and family therapy, or family sociology may add new learning and skills with which to improve litigation towards more rational mediation and arbitrated results. For instance, there is no requirement for the legal profession and the judiciary to have studied child or human development before assuming their decisive roles when parents separate. Though continuing education for the legal profession is offered in all or most of the states, there is not a uniform requirement that continuing education units be earned; nor is there a uniform requirement dictating what those courses need be.

Psychologist and author, Judith Wallerstein stated to me in an interview that, a number of years prior, she taught several courses in family psychology when on staff at the San Francisco State University School of Law.[231] As psychology was not a prerequisite for attending law school, the courses were offered as an important means for new attorneys to study interpersonal dynamics. Though she taught psychology for only a short while, Wallerstein said attorneys called her in subsequent years to say how much they appreciated her course. They would never have encountered psychological studies in any formal law school requirement and would seldom find it as a continuing education option.

Former chief justice Louis Brandeis is credited with saying, "Law without compassion is not justice."[232] Perhaps by delving with compassion into the plight of parents and children of divorce, the purposes of law in today's family courts will be better served.

Educating decision makers in the family court system is a prerequisite for more compassionate orders that may affect improved outcomes for dismantling families. A formal educational process can include contemporary legal, social science, and medical research. Additionally, family specialists as guest lecturers can be featured in continuing education programs. Accordingly, this process may expand the perceptions of family court professionals to accept the range of negative outcomes related to child access orders not enforced.

Is it reasonable to expect that family member outcomes will improve with more comprehensive professional training? According to social research, "To the extent that training increases knowledge of effective practices, enhances confidence in performing them, and decreases perceived obstacles ... the training program should produce positive changes in practice behavior."[233] The authors suggest that this training will be most successful when the professional expects that new skills will increase their effectiveness and productivity. Importantly, acceptance of these practices by national accrediting and professional organizations will strengthen new adaptations.

Thus, with continued vocational and professional development, there may ultimately be further prevention of damage to the children of divorce or, as Darnall refers to them, the "divorce casualties."[234]

Building upon Community Assets

Historically in America and among indigenous populations, there is reverence for the elders. The American community in general shows reverence post-mortem. Buildings are named for a deceased, formerly prominent political leader who, during his or her tenure, felt the undulations of a voting and vocal populace during many landslide and close elections.

Elders were important during the early days of American colonization and settlement. Today, it is not often the elder whom we look to or even respect. Instead, it is the family professional to whom the family in crisis turns. Therefore, the FP has extraordinary responsibilities but also unlimited opportunities to mitigate damage that families may face when parents choose to separate.

These professionals may find that regular education on new research, government reports and interdisciplinary findings may help them in their practices. Continuing education and professional schooling may help them

- obtain new knowledge,
- increase empathetic understanding,
- learn how each profession approaches the divorce process, and
- understand how FPs can become more effective practitioners as a result of this learning process.

The Workplace as Community Resource

The workplace offers separated or divorced individuals to be with others who may offer information and support during their crises.

Some are eager to share, to educate, to comfort. Some coworkers will commiserate; others may themselves become depressed by their stressed colleague. Other fellow employees ignore the situation, trying instead to focus on their own job responsibilities. These coworkers cannot provide the professional guidance that a divorcing parent requires.

There are different services that companies might provide to their employees, based on the risk factors and number of potentially vulnerable employees. These services may not be deterrents to the ensuing family litigation process. However, there are company-sponsored programs and policies that may serve as excellent interventions in reducing employee stress on and off the job. "Different employees will respond differently to divorce. Some move on with their lives relatively quickly. But the likelihood of severe or long-lasting stress is high, so it's wise to remind *all* [author's italics] divorcing employees about the support services your company provides."[235]

Depending on the company's size and human resource assets, employee assistance will vary. As mentioned earlier, the employee assistance program (EAP) is a program that some companies may subscribe to that provides employees with advice, referrals, and mental health services. Some companies may have on hand a list of community resources in their human resources department or in their employee handbook. But often, a company will not know which employee might be experiencing marital problems, or divorce, custody, or visitation difficulties. Therefore, web-based information might be helpful for those seeking information online through their corporate website.

Andrews and others caution against support groups onsite.[236] Their fear is that some employees may share too much personal information while others may not want to engage with fellow employees at all. A company might best help an employee by acknowledging their personal difficulties and providing flex time in his work schedule. Additional assistance may include

- educational seminars,
- individual professional consultations,

- conference calls,
- webcasts,
- lending libraries, and
- corporate newsletters.

As divorce and single parenting continues to remain at very high rates, companies may be motivated by production costs and bottom line profits to monitor individual productivity and absenteeism. Providing numerous and adequate workplace interventions will benefit employees whose work becomes impacted by their family breakdown, separation, and divorce. Therefore, whatever an employer may do to control this sociological phenomenon will be in the best interests of all—children, parents, and employer.

Summary Assessment for Change

The changes that occur, once there is a motion for divorce (in the case of a married couple) and custody (in the case of cohabiting couples), threaten to overwhelm the individuals involved. Emotional upsets easily interfere with one's day-to-day functioning. Relocation of domicile, child access, and redefined custody roles all affect parents' and children's daily routines.

Think of it in this manner: you've just parachuted from an airplane that provided food, toilets, shelter, and order. You don't know exactly where you are going to land. You have no information about weather, topography, and resources. You don't know the language. Regardless of the motivation for that "leap" from the plane, you have been dropped into a vast unknown. Sure, you may find a park ranger below or a city policeman. But are you assured of help down below? Indeed, are you assured of any assistance as you plummet toward a foreign environment?

Consider, again, that this is a jump that you may not have expected to make. But consider, too, that the parachute represents the means for the change from plane to new territory—an attorney if you will. The parachute is what the jumper expects will provide a safe transport into a new personal landscape. Though expensive, the parachute is, for many, their first thought. An inexperienced jumper may break a leg upon landing. The parachute, also, may not have been properly secured to the jumper's torso or may not have been packed well. The parachute may also unexpectedly collapse around the jumper, bringing the transition to an immediate end.

When those with children or property enter the dismantling stage of their relationship, it is often a reality that descends without warning, as did the need for the parachute above. A friend or relative refers one to an attorney for help because it is through the courts that civil matters are usually resolved. Custodial parents fear lost household income, plan reprisals for divorce filings, and seek to control child access. Frequently during this period, it is a mystery to the noncustodial parent why the custodial parent is requesting money and/or limited access to the children of the union. It is bewildering that restraining orders appear, along with allegations of domestic partner violence and sexual abuse of children.

Braver asserts that family violence accusations increase within six months before the couples separate.[237] He calls this period "the emotional peak," and it is evidenced by pushing, shoving, and throwing incidents. According to Braver, "these acts of violence are due to the extreme emotional stress of the moment and, for individuals with no history of abuse, may be unlikely to recur."[238] His study shows that reports of violence initiated by wives and those initiated by husbands decrease by half following separation with less than 4 percent requiring any medical attention.

Authors Maccoby and Mnookin advise that legal decisions in custody and visitation matters should exclude such evidence from these determinations.[239] They believe like Braver that in many cases abuse is alleged in order to better position one's argument before a judge. The problem is that these allegations are not tried until after the restraining order is imposed, often weeks later. Then the judge may still want to modify visitation for safety considerations or delay visitation motions until the temporary restraining order period is complete, usually eight to twelve weeks. The children are likewise victims of restraining orders, valid or false. Their emotions continue to be held hostage.

If we examine why people accuse, it is usually because of fear— fear of being dominated and fear of loss. Where does fear come from? If we realize that fear is a factor in the illogic of much of family court litigation, and if we see that fear comes from lack of knowledge, then it becomes a logical matter to fight fear with education. The mission for parents is not first to resolve their differences, but first to *acknowledge* their differences—

- acknowledge that each other has differing views,
- seek an understanding of why each has differing views, and
- find some bridge (mediation) to acceptance of these views.

The above process is not easy. But it can be completed with education. One does not attempt new education unless there is some compelling reason such as recreational need, income need, and spiritual need. Recreation helps one recover from business and personal stresses. Income enables one to meet basic survival needs. Spirituality help strengthen one's relationships with community through belief in life's purpose and continuity through this generation and the next as well as from those before. But it is with both heart and attitude that one can acknowledge, accept, and cope with communal and personal changes. Coping skills are seldom taught, though they should be. Such skills should be available through any family or community professional. Emotional strength and "practice" increases an individual's means to survive the traumatic upheavals that accompany dismantled love relationships.

FUTURE IMPLICATIONS AND PROTOCOLS FOR CHANGE

There is no reliable data from the courts that document race and educational level as variables in family custody decisions. Such data would be very helpful when looking at the recommendations of family relations/family services departments of the courts and orders by court judges and magistrates. Such data would help to refine public policy initiatives for improved co-parenting, particularly with respect to cultural norms.

The fact is that custody is one of the most sensitive and litigated issues in divorce, contributing to the hostility between some 30 percent of divorcing parents. Attorneys have confided in off-the-record conversations that these parents are "troublesome," to say the least. If we infer that one million children are affected annually by the divorce of their parents, we can say that 300,000 children each year are likely emotionally hurt, even abused, by one or the other parent. U.S. Census data show that "in 1998, 27.5 percent of children under age 18 were residing with a single parent, usually a single mother (84.1 percent), and about 11 percent had a nonresident, divorced or separated father. These figures have remained about similar since the 1990s with minor fluctuations."[240]

A strong minority of parents is believed to be alienating their children. The courts need to use their power to control this phenomenon when it is demonstrated by forensic psychological evaluation or other observations. When a child refuses to see or speak with their nonresidential parent, this will often be a reflection of the custodial parent's desire to sever all contact with the absent parent. The custodial parent's anger and pain of partnership loss overrides the need for the child to retain their bond with the other parent. Dr. Cheryl Lee found that custodial parents in these cases wanted to keep full control and power over divorce or separation and would do so by punishing the other parent by denying access to their children.[241]

More and more, social scientists and government researchers are relating socioeconomic variables such as level of education, household income, domestic violence history, and alcohol and drug abuse, to sole custody and joint custody (or co-parenting) awards. But it may be reasonable to correlate parental attitudes, self-perceptions, and behaviors to state policy makers who wish to advocate more equitable decisions for child custody and child access.

Behavior is the subject of sociological studies. Observations are documented in research studies, and no matter how close the standard deviations and correlates of isolated independent variables a study selects, it must be remembered that we are talking about people. These people carry out actions that might be statistically predictable. But statistics will be of greater use to policy makers when social scientists can demonstrate causality and motivation.

When sole custody is awarded more frequently than joint custody, is it because one parent has a home? Is it because that parent is a stay-at-home parent? Is it because that parent has a higher income? When we find that 80 percent of these custodial parents are mothers, can it be believed that their incomes are greater than that of the fathers'? That they are not working? That *their* home environment is better?

When the federal government and various studies reveal that children have a greater chance to thrive over the long term when both parents are involved in their lives, can we continue to accept the majority of cases in which sole custody is awarded? For instance, Connecticut has the highest rate of joint custody, at 48 percent.[242] But this still represents less than half of the custody awards in the state. Does this fact show that work still needs to be done?

We need to examine the assessments that are used by court systems when awarding custody and visitation. It will be invaluable to obtain those criteria that are used by judges when adjudicating.

But let us not forget the impact of depressive thought and behavior that can easily manifest when a loving relationship between any two people—in this case parents—ends. Should external quantitative measures be the sole basis for decisions made by legal authorities?

Attending to children's needs is difficult while dealing with the emotionally draining and physically exhausting logistics of court preparation. Court orders for child custody and especially child access should be monitored closely by the court. Parents' fury for control is most pronounced—and potentially most damaging to the child—in matters related to child access. The complexity of these decisions prompts consideration of alternative means for settling custody and child access matters, if not divorce. The unified courts had been advanced by the American Bar Association as a standard for more effective decision-making.[243] It is in the unified court where one judge and one courtroom are assigned to a case through the completion of all legal matters will likely produce more appropriate outcomes for children. Families who are heard by such a judge or magistrate will know the case, its history, the personalities, the issues and the arguments. It therefore would be expected that parents may then find more acceptable, or fair, judgments forthcoming.

New Paradigms: A Case for Court-Based Intervention

The American Bar Association notes that "the lack of communication between courts and social service agencies results in unnecessary delay, duplication, and contradictory rulings and recommendations."[244]

Consider that the unified court may be the place to first hear charges of abuse, including requests for restraining orders. Here, such charges can be seen and better understood in the context of a parent's disagreement with a temporary custody award or move-away restraint. The unified court will keep a family's file and proceedings assigned to the same judge or magistrate who heard the original motions and has come to know the case and all the parties including the plaintiff, the defendant, the children, and their respective counsel. Stability and continuity can then be enjoyed by the litigants who do not have to rehash, restate, or reintroduce testimony and evidence. Additionally, should this judge find that the allegations are deserving of, for example, probate, dependency, juvenile or criminal investigations, then parents can be referred to appropriate venues.

How about the training of family service caseworkers? Is it enough to have a specialist or two lead a discussion of parental alienation syndrome or child development once a year? What are the job qualifications for caseworkers? What are their own prejudices and fears when it comes to assisting families during their court experiences?

Is there any concern for the reactions of parents to the court process? In my many consultations with several hundred parents through the Children's Rights Council, I learned that (adult) parents feel powerless and helpless in court. Deferring to their attorney, they can simply react to court experiences that they believe are beyond their ken and control. However, a client debriefing with an assigned "parent advocate" might provide the information that the litigant needs.

CHAPTER 7

PROGRAM FOR CHANGE

PROJECT FACT: A COURT RESOURCE PROGRAM (FAMILIES AND CHILDREN IN TRANSITION)

A Court Resource Program

Project FACT:
Families and Children in Transition

History And Overview

In as much as nearly one half of all family cases including divorce and child custody are pro se (client representing self), and in as much as there is a need for attorneys to be expedient in the 'prosecution' of their cases, a new and helpful strategy is now needed in Family Courts across the country.

Such a significant strategy to provide families with emotional support and practical guidance can be implemented in courts around the country with modification of current court administration policy. I have constructed this unique program as Project FACT: Families and Children in Transition. It is based on the work of the Toby Center for Family Transitions (The Toby Center), a holistic service agency I founded to help families in change with information, child access and visitation services, and treat individuals clinically to affect improved outcomes for parents and children in transition.

As the research and discussion presented show, children, parents, indeed all extended family members will better adapt to their changed family structure when it becomes clear that the needs of family members will be best met by their implementation.

Project FACT was inspired by a New York City court administration program called Project LIFT, an acronym for Learning Information for Family Members, Family Professionals Training. This program was designed to provide information in English and Spanish for litigants in family court. Advisors conversant in both English and Spanish offer translation assistance with completing court documents and navigating the required paperwork for litigation and record keeping. Project LIFT functions as a court-based service to acclimate diverse populations to the correct use of the court system.

Its supporters claim that the service helps to reduce the cultural and language challenges faced by litigants in the family courts. Trained court administrative staff assist with forms, directions to courtrooms, and referrals to bilingual attorneys or other services.

The New York City program is unique and it does fulfill an important community function. Yet the program provides little more than translation services, preprinted documents in major foreign languages representing the populations being served, and occasional guidance from attorneys with some foreign language proficiency.

Remember that litigation and court experience can be traumatic, painful, and confusing for parents. This system presents itself a mysterious, cultural experience that requires increased attention to both practical and emotional needs of the litigating parents journeying through this. For those with counsel, they often feel uneasy after court appearances because of the legal vocabulary, legal process, and the dark, sparse room setting. There is seldom any time for attorneys to debrief their clients as they may have concurrently scheduled other client representations in the same court, or they need to return to their office.

Those appearing pro se have enough difficulty maneuvering through court processes without struggling to sort through their own impressions of the process and emotional reactions. For these people, financial pressures and inexperience compound their personal difficulties.

Project FACT is an adaptation of the Toby Center wraparound program which offers informational, educational, and support services to parents who are angry, fearful and often traumatized at this time in their lives.

PROJECT FACT: A CENTER FOR FAMILY CHANGE

Through an easily designed structure, the Project FACT model is in reality a 'center for family change' with the mission to deescalate conflict between parents, and demystify the legal constructs and processes that await many in family court.

Project FACT will achieve this through the requirement that all parents participate in an orientation seminar once they have initially served legal papers for divorce, or have received these documents. This orientation will personally introduce each parent to the Family Court system, procedures and expectations. Each Project FACT Center will dispense general instructions, guidelines and support to those seeking legal separation, divorce procedures, and child custody considerations.

In cases where domestic violence is reported, documented and pending criminal charges, the Court's Domestic Violence Advocate may be an important facilitator in addressing these issues. As we learned from Braver earlier, the potential for domestic abuse is greatest six months before and six months following divorce. Domestic violence needs to be addressed in a unique way because of frequent dual diagnoses as personality disorders among the parties often accompany addictions also present. Also, where children have been witnesses to these events will require special unique discussions for the parties.

Cultural and ethnic considerations can better be explained when language and behavior can be processed through face to face orientations facilitated by a family professional sharing the culture, the language, the ethnicity. New immigrant populations will benefit from such orientations which are personal, hands on, and where nuances can be addressed through immediate language and explanation.

The Project FACT goal is to help parents cope with family change brought about through the judicial system, necessary for orderly and documented steps in their divorce and child custody cases. Project FACT will provide onsite services that are immediately accessible and vital. Such onsite services in advance of attorney involvement, court appearances and family and or social service investigations or home studies will help clarify for parents the many services that they want and need, can't afford or don't know where to obtain information about. It will provide them with information and guidance they could not easily locate or afford.

The benefits for adopting a Project FACT in circuit courts are significant for Court administration and for potential criminal behaviors. These benefits are expected to:

1. Reduce court hearing time.
   Parties will be prepared for court procedure, including process for delivering motions and hearing requests.

2. Reduce returning court caseload.
   Court process and expectations will have been explained, and options for mediation and discussion are noted as acceptable objectives for otherwise combative parents.

3. Shortens court appearances.
   Focus on the case issue summaries which may be introduced during the court hearing would be more effectively constructed because of the guidelines explained by the Court in the orientation seminar. This will eliminate the lengthy and costly expense of litigation. Court protocols which allow introduction of reports and evaluations by court appointed or court approved psychotherapists will assure Family Court judges and magistrates of appropriate options in their decision making. Such a process will reduce further the need for further arbitration and court appearances.

4. Project FACT can accommodate more reasonable employment of family attorneys.
   Family attorneys who wish may find themselves more available for more clients by serving in consultative positions within the Clerk's office or other designated area. Working by appointment and likely available same day, this legal help will serve as immediate interventions to reduce or eliminate the potential for increased hostility, hostile behaviors, and

extreme actions including child abduction, partner and child murder, and suicide.

STRATEGIC GOALS OF PROJECT FACT

1. Reduction of unmanageable court caseload.
2. Reduction of returning caseload.
3. Helping parents craft agreements specific to their perceived needs without the pressure of opposing attorneys and subsequent repercussions (as domestic and family violence, stalking, etc).
4. Reduction of risk of parental physical and emotional harm.
5. More clarity and understanding by parents of child custody and access decisions.
6. More fluidity in resolving family litigation matters.
7. Reduction in stress for family litigants.
8. Reduction in stress for those adjudicating.
9. More efficient hearings.
10. Less family and domestic violence.
11. Less juvenile crime.
12. Fewer teen pregnancies.
13. Less job absenteeism (as this often accompanies depression).
14. Increased educational achievement.

REASONS FOR PROJECT FACT

In many courthouses, there are few opportunities for litigants to receive information, education, and support. There are seldom waiting rooms with comfortable chairs or sofas for reading, relaxing, or contemplation prior to or following court appearances. Absent more attention from one's attorney following their hearing, additional court services may prove very helpful.

Project FACT can educate litigants through pre- and

post-court appearances. The service offers realistic but compassionate explanations of the court process. Funded or volunteer staff members could offer onsite, private assistance to those requesting the service. Legal interpretations and directions may be provided by pro bono attorneys. Professional social workers and healthcare providers could offer other interventions and referrals. Staffing can be through internships and may even be serviced by professionals who will receive continuing education units in states where continuing education is mandated for their professions.

Project FACT is an easily adaptable program designed to lend assistance to parents journeying through a long, lonesome, and vexing court process. Who is there to reassure the parties during the "great wait" in the court lobby and court pews? Few can offer kindly support during a litigant's actual court appearance and, particularly, the long walk from the bench to the exit.

Litigants' needs are both immediate and urgent. They need an understanding of the court process in which they are now engaged; they require advice to "stay" their focus on the legal issues at hand as the court may require; they need help in strategizing their case and as yet unheard or unresolved issues. Litigants also need emotional interventions. Their fears and concerns need validation. Anxiety, anger, and hopelessness may cause self-inflicted emotional and or physical injury, particularly when the courts are used to resolve child access issues. Worse still, these negative emotions may drive litigants to endanger other family members.

Project FACT is designed to provide individuals with comfort and empowerment by helping to replace those feelings with acceptance and understanding and control. Unlike existing court services, Project FACT was designed to help better transition children and parents emotionally as well as practically by providing them with one or more onsite consultants. Onsite consultants would provide assistance to each family court litigant who asks for this support. Protocols include physical and spiritual guidance during the protracted and probably very expensive court process. Divorce litigants will be provided research, guidance, and referrals for their existing needs, and at no cost. This information shall address any and all concerns including medical, psychological, and social.

How Project FACT Will Help Parents

Project FACT will include multiple services:

1. Procedural guidance;
2. Information about how and when to communicate with attorneys;
3. Explanation of the role of family court in identifying family complaints;
4. Suggestions about how best to use the courts and alternatives for resolving conflict;
5. Personal acknowledgment of the litigant's pain, confusion, fear, and anger that often accompanies, festers, and sometimes overcomes the individual litigant;
6. Referrals to community resources including help with:
    a. Job training and education,
    b. Support group and psychological referrals,
    c. Basic instruction in personal budgeting including child support, and
    d. Assistance with child custody and access/visitation concerns.

How Project FACT Will Help Attorneys

Project FACT will benefit attorneys in the following ways:

1. Relieving attorneys of the emotional care of their litigants;
2. Providing guardian *ad litems* with current research related to shared parenting, child custody, and child access;
3. Providing mediation assistance;

4. Providing information on evolving family law policy issues nationally;
5. Providing referrals to community resources and other parts of the country where case information, litigants, or children reside; and
6. Explaining how to identify the emotional issues as they relate to predictable behavior models.

THE PROJECT FACT CENTER FOR FAMILY TRANSITION

FAMILY KNOWLEDGE CENTER

Today, the most valuable free supports for litigants found in courts are instruction pamphlets in English and Spanish or other languages spoken in the district served. It remains a do-it-yourself approach for family court litigants. An occasional translator will have office time. Seldom is a computer accessible with links to information about court functions, community resources, or self-care.

With the advent of computer technology over twenty years ago and the escalating advance of social media, self-learning has become a momentous, instantaneous opportunity for learning. The challenges do remain as to the authenticity and reliability of information that is found and shared. However, the access to periodical literature, research and policy is an invaluable means to prepare and choose when one's world is caving in. The Family Knowledge Center, described below, offers all individuals that opportunity.

The concept of helping families survive their trauma of parental separation and divorce is borrowed from a successful audiovisual library at the Massachusetts General Hospital in Boston. I found this "Health Library" when my mother, Toby, was seriously ill and hospitalized there.

With my sister, Dr. Janet Roseman, we examined the value of multiple modalities in self concept, independent learning, and access to resources. Integration of such resources have the most effectiveness in improving one's own ability to adapt to current conditions and control for the outcomes one would prefer.

Such a facility that can provide this Center offers individuals an extraordinary opportunity for professional atmosphere, independent study, and privacy.

What impressed me at Mass General was access to resources that may not be easily available to many people. In fact, Toby Center staff found that some 35-40% of families haven't the funds for critical and vital child access, mediation, or therapeutic services. Though many do have cell phones with internet data capacity, they do not have the guidance for obtaining resources mentioned above. The Family Knowledge Center will provide this as long as there is also a staff member trained in guiding people to the appropriate websites for information.

Let's review this Center concept further, with the recognition, too, that parents enduring divorce and child custody are entering the unknown legal arena. For many, they are shell shocked and frightened. They need guidance to endure and achieve what for many will be valuable custody arrangements for their children.

With establishment of an informational and service resource as Project FACT in each metropolitan area, I am confident we can provide more resilience among those most emotionally fragile at this time in their lives. I am confident, too, that we shall improve the relationships between parents post divorce. We will also find that children will be more reassured of protection and love.

I urge communities, Circuit Courts, municipal governments, even the Bar Associations and Mental Health Membership Organizations to establish a Center in their regional communities. It is a proven concept. What I find so extraordinary about Mass General's Center concept is that it was designed by those who would use the facility, including health professionals, patients, their families, and other interested citizens. It truly is a communal asset and extraordinarily designed by those who would most benefit from it use.

The library is lined with shelves containing publications for professional and lay readers. There are Internet-ready computers that provide access to proprietary, research, and subscription health databases. The library has tables with outlets for personal laptops, private study carrels, and a private area for viewing videos, complete with headphones. Such resources are powerful opportunities for self-study as families cope with new and challenging health conditions (and choices) that they and their loved ones must face.

This model might well be used to assist parents experiencing separation and divorce. Such a family knowledge center might prove extremely valuable to parents, children, grandparents, and other extended family members during these vulnerable times. The center would offer information in various formats such as audio, visual, and computer-based. There would be individual study cubicles to enable privacy, and conference rooms for more formalized dialogue and presentations. Books and journals would be available for individuals who search for answers to new questions. Volunteers might also make referrals to community resources, child and adult mentors, and, perhaps, lend an ear. Such human interactions can validate the individual's difficult journey and support their adaptation and recovery.

The Toby Center for Family Transitions, Inc. based in Florida has developed the Project Fact Service Model. This model is designed to provide rapid and low cost visitation and therapeutic services and depends upon low overhead strategies to accomplish that. Most of Toby Center facilities are donated from the faith-based community, and through low cost rental arrangements with nonprofit agencies. A sliding scale fee structure makes services more affordable, and especially helps those who are unable to use health insurance for behavioral health services and supervised parenting (visitation) sessions.

Project FACT locations would offer convenient and accessible resources to save children's emotional and physical lives.

EPILOGUE

A Common Understanding

In this television culture where programs of trial law, forensic science, and investigation seem to occupy evening viewing hours, viewers are shown, as in myths, that good can overcome evil. These shows attract viewers through their portrayal of realistic scenarios. However, it may be unrealistic for a viewer to conclude (as their favorite show may demonstrate) that victims or their survivors can obtain justice and that, ultimately, the punishment will fit the crime.

For many in divorce or family court, the above is not the case. The superabundance of negative effects upon children when their parents separate provide the motivation for examining the role of existing interventions, including dependency on the courts to resolve custody and visitation problems.

There are so many negative messages attacking a parent when the family is dismantling that it is hard to know where and how to begin to cope with the issues at hand. When parents separate, different parts of their being become vulnerable. One's emotional spirit is depressed, and companionship may be lacking. One remains lost in a new world where little makes sense and even more is not at all understood.

The urgency for society to adopt more positive, empowering, and supportive interventions presents itself when parents choose to separate. Generally, a parent has no idea what issue to address first. From the data presented, it can be concluded that negative, even hostile, feelings and a poor self-image may interfere with the process of prioritizing the issues that need to be settled when parents choose to separate.

Let me summarize events upon divorce and custody action which can be chaotic and yet, pose opportunities for improved outcomes.

When parents first separate, one has likely already engaged an attorney for advice and or counsel. A subpoena is most often delivered to the defendant party who will likely become the non custodial parent. The subpoena will contain notification for divorce and or child custody hearing, and temporary orders for child access may also be included or shortly argued.

In the hundreds of court orders that I have read across jurisdictions while working at CRC and in reviewing the hundreds of client court orders the Toby Center receives from clients, I have found it so unfortunate that these imposing documents should be frequently so incomplete. They are written without specific details for shared parenting, supervised visitation, child exchange or decision making responsibilities.

In those few states where mediation is required, the MSA's (Marriage Settlement Agreements) may be created including or with attached parenting plans. In spite of the efforts at detail, these frequently lack very important instructions relating to many circumstances outside of the 'cookie cutter' alternative weekend visitation schedules. Consider the following:

- the custodial and guardian needs of children in transit, when visitation betweens parents necessitate mass transportation;
- that both parents be deemed contacts in event of emergency;
- that the non custodial parent be called first should the primary parent has a scheduling conflict for work related travel, social event or other need;
- both parents need to be on formal record with schools, camps, church and synagogue, medical and hospital records, passports, all formal documents.

It is neither practical, nor is it sensible that as parenting time be limited solely to agreed upon co-parenting schedules. I would argue a child would prefer their available parent to in fact, 'parent' the child instead of having a baby sitter.

It is a serious oversight when a parent, usually the non custodial (non-residential, or 'absent') parent is excluded from such documentation. It is harmful to the child who may learn that they 'cannot call that parent' in event of emergency. Such oversight, such ignorance purports that the child is not important to that parent, that *other* parent whom they also, love.

This text is further based on documented, practical, and first-hand experience of professionals in law, therapy, human service organizations, child advocates, academic research, public policy and medicine.

Therefore, the goals of this author have been to help the litigating parents, their representatives and all family professionals with new understandings of how shared dialogue might improve the lives of parents, children, and extended family members following the restructuring of their dual-parent home.

Preserving Family Ties is written with love for family values and the belief that families can withstand increasing environmental pressures, given new social systems designed to support that resiliency.

Yet, there are systems that we cannot avoid when one or both parents decide they want to divorce. The intrusiveness and controls of litigation, the discomfort and stigma of therapy (for men especially), the changed relationships with children all 'conspire' to torture and scar us. We become highly sensitized, with embarrassment, sadness, and fear.

So, what to do? We often retreat from friends, and also, from family. Divorce is so difficult to find trusting sources of support, those who understand it, and who have experienced it. Those who have will likely find such groups to improve their coping ability for this life changing event.

COPING WITH DIVORCE

Oddly, support groups attract more women than men. Perhaps this explains why second marriages have a higher failure rate. Most in second marriages do not "do the work" for their own personal growth. They blame the other person from the first marriage and don't learn of their own complicity in the collapse of their earlier relationship. So, where can one turn for help?

For me, I was so fortunate to find For Men Only, a men's support group in Branford, Connecticut. It was for me most important in restoring confidence. Members cared, listened to each other, they heard me, and helped me through their reflection, and insight. Older, more experienced men grounded me in my angry, disappointing world view. They encouraged me in my departure from financial services to my child advocacy work in Washington. Members admired my enrollment in a doctoral program. They welcomed my dates at their social events.

When support groups are unavailable, start one.

For most, then, bookstores and online web sites provide immediate information for self-help. However, observations in many large and small bookstores reveal an absence of specific sections relating to the "divorce experience."

There are stores that do sell books covering the subject of divorce, custody, and visitation in self-help, marriage, children, relationships, and pop psychology such as John Gray's *Men Are from Mars, Women Are from Venus*. There are books written from the father's perspective, a mother's perspective, and many with the aim to 'win' in court. There are books to help one avoid custody battles, and those increasingly to discover mindful and collaborative divorce.

But it can be quite difficult to locate in stores and libraries specific information about issues facing many American families today. It is quite troubling, especially for those individuals who struggle with great pain to enter, alone, as victims with little energy, into a large book retailer seeking answers that are so well hidden.

More bookstores seem to carry titles about gender-specific

self-representation in court and litigation tactics. Titles aim to improve communication between parents and understand children's fears. Yet observations show that self-published and mass-market autobiographies of triumph or loss or hope fill more bookshelves and Internet web sites each year.

Single parents, therapists, stepmoms, and others participating in the crusade to maintain, strengthen, or reunify children with their noncustodial parents, have written many books in the last ten years. Many of them are self-published; others are distributed through mainstream publishers. However, they all tell of experiences, stories, advice, and recommendations. Among the more popular authors are Warren Farrell, with his gentle discourse on how to unite dads and children, in *Father and Child Reunion;* and Lynne Oxhorn-Ringwood and Louise Oxhorn as mother and stepmother in *Step-Wives,* with frank instructions for establishing a safe and loving relationship with children shared between moms and stepmoms. Two premier books that should be bookshelf standards on shared parenting were written by family court attorneys, Michael Oddendino's *Putting Kids First,* and David Levy's *The Best Parent Is Both Parents.*

Yet, for many, books which may be found may confuse, may steer one towards the author's direction, and not the direction most appropriate, most practical, one that is best for the individual.

As those parents separating and divorced today, my journey was a new learning experience. I had little knowledge of divorce and child custody, the legal process, family change and the associated and abrupt psychological effects. Few do.

I found the divorce landscape marred by craters of financial and emotional wounds, so deep and filled with tears. I attended conferences on parenting, classes on family law, and searched for support groups and professional associations where I could obtain particular insights into the nature and breadth of divorce and family change.

Subsequently, I grew professionally, working in Washington on family issues, walking the halls of the U.S. Congress, and meeting families all around the country. I grew academically as a doctoral student where I found new learning to help me design programs I have implemented and more that research shows will help us all as parents and as family professionals to improve outcomes for children.

Given this personal, professional experience and academic research, I have identified three knowledge-based curriculum goals. These are goals which, if we can bring to graduate programs in law, psychology, and mental health, we should be able to holistically train family professionals across disciplines and therefore, affect improved service delivery to achieve improved outcomes for children. These educational goals are:

1. Appreciation for each profession's unique abilities;
2. Comprehension of how different professionals can work synergistically;
3. Practical advice for implementing new interventions and protocols into the subject priorities and learning methods valued by family professionals.

If we can integrate these overall goals in professional training and certification requirements, we can improve our judicial and social responses. If we remember and apply the processes of the civil rights movement, namely debate, support and a willingness to accept our differences, then we can channel our efforts towards the benefits of the society at large. Then, successful transformation and social change can best occur.

Today, there are more variations of divorce settlements including the use of mediation to enable parents to better determine their own terms. For highly conflicted parents, some states have approved the use court approved parent coordinators who are usually therapists able to manage hostility and intransient parties. There has been success with this more expensive alternative to litigation.

Increasingly also is collaborative divorce, where parents work with a team comprising a therapist, an attorney, a Guardian Ad Litem and a mediator. There are different team formats, but this procedure succeeds when both parties agree to be transparent with their financial information, and their goals.

Yet, as I've cited earlier, child custody is the most overriding and very frequently, the most fundamental and sobering focus when parents split. Why should it be that the most challenging, the most uncomfortable, and the most heart wrenching task is that of the division of parenting responsibilities, support, and decision making? The welfare of their children is the most divisive and most fragile of conversations which can threaten, which can harm, and which knock most everyone's future off a stable track.

It is you, the parents, and you the professionals who must create your own road map for child rearing. As I stated in the Preface, this book will not provide you with the resolution you may need for divorce and child custody issues. It is to be your guide to enlighten parents and family professionals about the myriad of trappings, traps, and history which will likely impact your divorce. You need to make important decisions which will affect so many whom you love, whom you no longer love, whom you know, and whom you don't know.

Whether a therapist, an attorney, a minister, a parent, a grandparent, a friend, the reader must understand that there is no single panacea for divorce outcomes and children's welfare.

However, with the understanding of your state's family laws, the settlement options available in your state, your own wishes for raising your children, there are choices to be sought, negotiated, and litigated.

JOINT CUSTODY: ADVOCACY AND SUPPORT

Conversation about divorce and child custody would not be complete unless the reader understands that societal changes are frequently the result of political action through advocacy. I will discuss at length the role of the Children's Rights Council which influenced joint custody statutes internationally. CRC is also where I had worked with and learned much about child advocacy from David L. Levy, Esq.

Advocacy is the proactive effort to affect change by public demonstrations, conferences, personal conversations with political leadership, and sharing of information to those gatekeepers to agents of public policy change.

As cited earlier, the Children's Rights Council (CRC) was founded by a group of single parents including David Levy who sought to correct what was believed bias in the award of child custody in the 1980's when divorce cases began to increase and flood family courts. Professionals, these parents sought to create a valuable outlet to review child custody research, call for more investigation, and petition for joint custody options in family courts around the United States. Over time, the CRC became well respected internationally and helped provide research which parenting groups from the United Kingdom, Canada, Australian and France used in their petitions for joint custody in their respective governments . I had the privilege to participate in fund raisings for the CRC held by the British and French Ambassadors in appreciation for David's leadership in the child custody movement.

David's vision as CRC's President served as a robust advocate for joint custody and spear headed changes in family law statutes of more than thirty states. His political activism, Congressional speeches, public appearances, and writings which led to David's increasing regional and national notoriety including appearances on shows as Dr. Phil, Oprah, interviews on Public Radio, and articles in the New York Times and the Washington Post.

As an advocacy organization, and under David's leadership, the CRC evolved from a group of thirty single dads and single moms and step parents without custody, and grandparents left out of child access agreements to a national organization of 2000 members.

Among these members were distinguished Board Members and supporters including Abigail Van Buren ('Dear Abby'), Karen DeCrow, President of New York Chapter of National Organization for Women, Author Dr. Warren Farrell, Dr. Judith Wallerstein and Dr.

Joan Kelly, pioneer family researchers on divorce and child outcomes. Teresa Kaiser, Esq. then Maryland Director of Human Resources, and Mike Oddendino, Esq., of California additionally helped create public policy based on their viewing firsthand the great and grave difficulties that children faced when parents divorced, particularly in high conflict divorce. They saw, too, the opportunities for improved in the American social fabric and the family professionals so integral within it.

Why was CRC so successful in achieving public recognition as advocate for policy changes to custody?

It is because during the 80's and 90's, the issues brought forth by the organization through national media and conferences were recognized by many in government and social agencies. That parents came from across social, economic, racial, educational, religious and professional sectors further gave credence to the cry that they all wished to remain involved in their children's lives. Most were appalled by their treatment in family court and were angered by their perception that in custody decisions, *fathers did not matter*. No longer should mothers be solely identified as the rightful providers of nurturing and protective care. It could now be argued it was now time to reverse this notion that fathers had no abilities to continue in their parenting role. It was time to reevaluate the nature vs. nurture argument, and to consider that fathers did indeed matter to their children.

They were equally distressed that moms were increasingly being victimized and barred from their children's lives. They feared that allegations of domestic abuse were most likely spurious tactics to assist in sole custody appointments and sought research to confirm the origin and use of domestic violence allegations. This was of particular concern because of frequent use of ex parte court orders often issued without options for defense testimony.

The advocacy efforts gave parents a voice, a voice that could be heard in various venues. In Connecticut where I was an active advocate for joint custody, newspapers, radio stations and television broadcasters eagerly responded to my offering to share research call for policy change.

I was subsequently recruited to serve on the Fatherhood Committee of the Governor's Commission on Divorce, Custody and Children where I had supported the Department of Social Service's suggestion for testimony about court procedure and joint custody decision making. This testimony became a marvelous twelve month campaign to gather data from professionals and parents from around the State of Connecticut to determine a) how agencies can collaborate; b) if family court system should institute changes; and c) to learn what advocates view as being in children's best interests.

At the conclusion of its review of the data, I was asked to speak as the representative of Connecticut's fathers when the State unveiled its report to Connecticut judges, family court administrators and family service representatives meeting at Quinnipiac University School of Law in 2002.

David was very impressed with my efforts in my home state. He had seen that though Connecticut led the U.S. in the 1990's with joint custody determinations, that such court orders were de facto as there was no joint custody statute in Connecticut. He was frequently in touch with Supreme Court Judge Anne C. Dranginis to discuss opportunities for joint custody legislation.

Why the need for child custody advocacy? Consider the research findings pointing to the fact that until the mid 1980's, family courts were deciding custody cases on older, 19th century traditional values which believed that the mother was the only party capable of adequately nurturing children.

During the late 1980's, the social phenomenon of divorce had been growing exponentially. There was now need for new sociological research and psychological studies to examine how and why courts continued to award custody to mothers. Disappointed fathers began to demonstrate outside of court houses, and on town greens becoming vocal, articulate, and declaring their value in child rearing and family outcomes.

The CRC focused on obtaining and sharing of new research which underscored children's emotional and social needs satisfied by both moms and dads. CRC began hosting annual conferences addressing joint custody and child outcomes and provided social scientists from academia and government the forum for important new research. As the research began to show that fathers were able to competently parent their children, that fathers were found important in their children's academic and social outcomes, then other organizations especially feminist ones felt threatened. It was CRC which invited these organizations to share in the research findings and work towards advocating more equitable state statutes on joint custody.

I was privileged to serve as CRC's conference manager, and helped create new forums for researchers, policy makers, family attorneys and forensic psychologists on the cutting edge of parenting philosophy. Increasingly, these conferences were expanded to include more of those professionals in the field who could benefit from the research and share in their own organization and agency's policy changes.

In the early 1990's during its growing popularity as a national advocacy, CRC created a supervised visitation program which was called CRC Child Access Services. This became the largest network of supervised visitation services in the nation with nearly 40 locations nationally. It grew because David secured funding from the Annie E. Casey foundation, and committed to meeting the needs of family court judges who rapidly embraced supervised visitation as the viable tool to protect and assure that a child can have a relationship with the parent who was not resident in their home.

When I joined CRC national as Assistant Director of Child Access, I helped expand CRC's recruitment of college students from around the country to increase CRC's studies and research of child outcomes. CRC's findings continued to support joint custody and received national attention.

When the Annie E. Casey Foundation learned of CRC's research, the Foundation agreed to provide partial funding for CRC's child access programming and then continued to publish their own child outcome measures each year. Casey's study continues to be the barometer for child outcomes today.

Similarly, in a wonderful coup for CRC, attorney Karen DeCrow, the Greater Syracuse Chapter President for NOW joined CRC, serving on the CRC Board for years. Following her passing, columnist Cathy Young attributed to DeCrow, an attorney and stalwart national figure for women's rights, as "this pioneer of modern feminism". (The Atlantic, *The Feminist Leader Who Became a Mens-Rights Activist*, June 2014). DeCrow felt that women's rights were not antithetical to parents' rights. and that '*the Best Parent is BOTH Parents*', the CRC tagline and title of David's book The Best Parent is Both Parents: A Guide to Shared Parenting in the 21st Century (Hampton Roads Publishing Company, Charlottesville, VA, 1998)

What makes a successful advocate?

Once meeting Dave, I knew that he was the man I wanted to emulate in behalf of children and as a humanist. I, too, wanted bring forth the new research, I wanted also to be an agent of change in a damaged world of family matters.

David was an orator. He loved people, he love to speak, he loved to educate. His grin and his laughter mesmerized audiences as he spoke of the rights of children to loving moms and dads. He was an unabashed humorist!

Upon meeting David in New York in 1999, David invited me as anyone else to visit the modest DC offices of the CRC. When I did so, repeatedly traveling from Connecticut to learn from him, he knew he had potential kin in child advocacy. Julie, David's office manager and former Congressional Staff Assistant on Capitol Hill, became an attorney through her own tenacity and determination to fight for parents rights. It was her kindness and dedication to the CRC mission which brought light to a small office doing great things.

David taught me the value of networking with the courts which I did throughout Baltimore and Washington, D.C. CRC press conferences at the Rayburn House Office Building announced new social research in shared parenting and child outcomes and international policy standards in child custody.

Importantly to note, it was David who petitioned the Clinton administration to allocate money to use in protecting the bonds of children and their single, separated, divorced and never married parents. He was successful through testimony on Capitol Hill and visiting influential Congressmen that the Federal Department of Health and Human Services introduced an annual distribution of funds for this purpose. Titled the Child Access and Visitation block grant, $1 million was fist set aside to states for visitation and mediation purposes. Further efforts by David during the George W. Bush Administration increased that expenditure to $10 million.

Over my years at CRC, I examined the role of mediation, of progressive visitation arrangements, of high conflict, and therapeutic visitation, all of which had contributed to the mitigation of alienation and blockading of non custodial parents by custodial parents. David introduced me to Washington policymakers and bureaucrats, and specialists who sought to improve child outcomes.

As I uncovered the benefits of educating divorced and separated parents, of networking with psychologists, school social workers and pediatricians, I realized that we all needed to work together in helping parents during their very trying, oft traumatic trials and separations. I therefore introduced to CRC conferences the work of CASA, the roles of school guidance counselors and well trained visitation facilitators in order to reduce the rancor and anger and fear experienced by parents and also their children. David trusted and encouraged me to invite these professionals from differing disciplines and expand our singular role as conduit of shared parenting policy, research and applications to improve child outcomes.

As individual parents, as family professionals, as educators, doctors, family judges and policymakers, we ought to think hard about those who may benefit from our work, and those who have influenced the work we do. An attorney, Dave believe that interdisciplinary approaches would be effective.

The success of an advocate is seen when one cannot separate the concepts of child access and co-parenting from their person. As Al, Dave passed in December 2014, having accomplished so very much in behalf children. I have harbored respect for David, admired his focus and dedication, and appreciated his love of family.

As Dave had used the American principles of democracy and legislation to affect improvement in state statutes and federal policy, law makers would be served well to consider cause and effect of child outcomes, both good and not.

They will be all be appreciated when child custody laws and court process will most reflect the innate desires of children to want both parents in their lives, and indeed, reflect that both parents are key to societal progress and preservation of family values.

BIBLIOGRAPHY

ABC's of Parenting: Guidelines for Access and Visitation Center. New Haven: New Haven Family Alliance, 2001.

Abraham, Jed H. *From Courtship to Courtroom: What Divorce Law Is Doing to Marriage.* New York: Bloch Publishing, 2000.

Ahrons, Constance. *The Good Divorce.* New York: Harper Collins, 2000.

Ahrons, Constance, and L. Wallisch. "Parenting in the Binuclear Family: Relationships between biological and stepparents. In *Remarriage and Step-parenting: Current Research and Theory,* ed. K. Paisley and M. Ihinger-Tallman. New York: Guilford Press, 1995.

Ahrons, Constance, and Richard Miller. "The Effect of the Post Divorce Relationship on Paternal Involvement: A Longitudinal Analysis." *American Journal of Orthopsychiatry* 63 (1993): 441–450.

Albistoma, C. R., Eleanor E. Maccoby, and Robert R. Mnookin. "Does Joint Legal Custody Matter?" *Stanford Law and Policy Review* 2 (2002): 167–179.

Amato, Paul and Cathryn Booth. "Children of Divorce: A Longitudinal Study." *Journal of Family Psychology* 55 (September 2001): 355–370.

Amato, Paul, and John Gilbreth. "Nonresident Fathers and Children's Well-Being: A Meta-Analysis." *Journal of Marriage and the Family* 61, no. 3 (1999): 557.

Ambert, Anne-Marie. *Divorce: Facts, Causes and Consequences.* Vamier Institute of the Family, rev. ed., 2005.

American Bar Association, "Family Law Changes to Alter Parenting," 7 January 2006, ABC News. http://www.abc.net.au/news/news/stories/2006/07/0/ 1676256.htm.

"An Overview of Florida's Criminal Justice Specialized Courts." *Florida Community Commission Report* 97 (October 1997): 231.

Andrews, Linda Wasmer. "Coping with Divorce." *HR Magazine* 50, no. 5 (2005): 61.

Arditti, Joyce A., and Katherine R. Allen. "Understanding Distressed Fathers' Perceptions of Legal and Relational Inequities Post-Divorce." *Family and Conciliation Courts Review* 31 (1993): 361.

Arnold, L. Eugene. *Childhood Stress.* New York: John Wiley and Sons, 2002.

Artis, Julie. "Judging the Best Interests of the Child: Judges Accounts of the Tender Years Doctrine." *Law Society Review* 38 (2004): 779.

Atkinson, James. *Joint Custody Determination*. Chicago, Il: American Association, 1996, http://www.abanet.org/family/faq.html, (accessed 10 January 1996).

Babor, Thomas F., John C. Higgins-Biddle, Pamela S. Higgins, Ruth A. Gassman, and Bruce E. Gould, MD "Training Medical Providers to Conduct Alcohol Screening and Brief Interventions." *Substance Abuse* 25, no. 1 (2004): 24.

Bacon, Brenda L., and Brad McKenzie. "Parent Education after Separation/Divorce: Impact of the Level of Parental Conflict on Outcomes." *Family Court Review* 42, no. 2 (2005): 263.

Bane, M. J. "Marital Disruption and the Lives of Children." *Journal of Social Issues* 32 (2002): 109–110.

Bauserman, Robert. "Child Adjustment in Joint-Custody Versus Sole-Custody Arrangements: A Meta-Analytic Review." *Journal of Family Psychology* 16, no. 1 (2002): 91–102.

Bennett, W. J. 1987. "The Role of the Family in the Nurture and Protection of the Young." *American Psychologist* 42: 246–250.

Berger, Joy, MD. "The Four Cornerstones of Healing 2004," unpublished manuscript, courtesy of Janet Roseman, PhD, 2003.

Best Interest of the Child Standard in Connecticut, Department of the Judiciary, State of Connecticut, 2005. http://w.ww.jud.ct.gov/ lawlib/notebooks/pathfinders/BestInterestsoftheChildStandard/ BestInterest.html.

Bienenfeld, Florence. *Helping Your Child Succeed After Divorce*. Claremont, California: Hunter House, 1987.

Block, Jeanne H., Jack Block, and Per. F. Gjerde. 1986. "The Personality of Children Prior to Divorce." *Child Development* 57: 827.

Blong, Detzner, Keuster, Eliason, and Allan, "Developing Culturally Sensitive Parent Education Programs for Immigrant Families: The Helping Youth Succeed Curriculum," *Hmong Studies Journal* 5 (2006): 1–29.

Blumner, Robyn. "Court-Ordered Sexism." *St. Petersburg Times.* 16 May 2004.

Bogenschneider, Karen. "Risk Focused Prevention of Juvenile Crime." *Child and Family Studies*, November 1994.

Borrell-Carrio, Francesc, M.D., Anthony L. Suchman, MD, and Ronald Epstein, MD. "Biopsychosocial Model 25 Years Later: Principles, Practice, and Scientific Inquiry." *Annals of Family Medicine* 2 (2004): 576–582.

Bradshaw, John, and J. Miller. "Lone Parent Families in the UK."*Her Majesty's Society of Orthopsychiatry* 18 (1991): 181.

Bramlett, Matthew, and William Mosher, "First Marriage Dissolution, Divorce, and Remarriage: United States," *Advance Data from Vital and Health Statistics* (May 2001): 323.

Braver, Sanford, and Diane O'Connell. *Divorced Dads, Shattering the Myth.* New York: Jeremy Tarcher/Putnam, 1998.

Bronfenbrenner, Urie. *The Ecology of Human Development.* Cambridge: Harvard University Press, 1979.

Bumpass, Larry L. James A. Sweet, and Andrew Cherlin. 1991. "The Role of Cohabitation in Declining Rates of Marriage." *Journal of Marriage and the Family* 53 (1991): 913.

Buscaglia, Leo. *Living, Loving and Learning.* New York: Ballentine Books, 1983.

Cancian, Maria, and Daniel R. Meyer. "Who Gets Custody?" *Demography* 35, no. 2 (1998): 147–157.

Cherlin, Andrew J. *The Changing American Family and Public Policy.* Washington, D.C.: Urban Institute Press. 1987.

_____. *Divorce and Remarriage.* Cambridge: Harvard University Press, 1992.

Child Custody. Divorced Families. U.S. Census Current Population Survey, 1997.

Chiriboga, David A., Linda S. Catron, and Associates, eds. *Divorce: Crisis, Challenge or Relief?* New York: New York University Press, 1991.

Clawar, S. S., and B. V. Rivlin. *Children Held Hostage: Dealing with Programmed and Brainwashed Children.* Chicago: American Bar Association, 1991.

Clinton, Hillary. Remarks at the Democratic National Convention. Associated Press, 27 August 1996.

Cohabitation, Marriage, Divorce and Remarriage in the United States 23, no. 22 (1998): 95.

Cohen, George J., MD. "Helping Children and Families Deal with Divorce and Separation." *Pediatrics* 110 (2002): 1019.

Cookston, Jeffrey T., Sanford L. Braver, Irwin Sandler, and M. Toni Genalo. "Prospects for Expanded Parent Education Services for Divorcing Families with Children." *Family Court Review* 40 (2002): 191.

Corcoran, Mary. "Non-resident Father Involvement and Child Well-Being: Can Dads Make a Difference?" *Journal of Family Issues* 15, no. 1 (1994): 96.

Cottrill, Jeffrey. "The State of the Union." *Divorce Magazine* 1, no. 3 (2004): 60.

Counseling. Washington, D.C.: Association of Catholic Charities, 2002, 3-9.

Creed of Healing. The Reiki Plus Institute of Natural Healing, 2004. http://www.reikiplus.com/news.html.

Darnall, Douglas. *Divorce Casualties: Protecting Your Children from Parental Alienation.* Dallas: Taylor Publishing, 1998.

DiCaro, Vincent. "With This Ring." *Fatherhood Today* 10, no. 3 (2005): 4–5.

Doherty, William, Edward Koneski, and Martha Farrell Erickson. "Noncustodial Parents' Participation in their Children's Lives: Evidence from the Survey of Income and Program Participation." *Report from the Fatherhood Initiative* (1998).

Dossey, Barbara, ed. *Holistic Nursing: A Handbook for Practice*, 3rd ed. Aspen: Aspen Publishers, 2000.

Dunn, Judy, et al. "Children's Relationships with Their Non-Resident Fathers." *Journal of Child and Adolescent Psychology* 45, no. 3 (2004): 566.

Dunne, John, and Marsha Hedrick. "The Parental Alienation Syndrome: An Analysis of Sixteen Selected Cases." *Journal of Divorce and Remarriage* 21, no. 3/4 (1994): 27.

Eaton, Janet. "Parenting Relationship after Divorce: Implications of Rationalization Regarding Well-being of Children." PhD diss., The Union Institute, 1998.

Ellis, Jane W. "Reconciling Discretion and Justice in Parenting Plan Disputes: The Washington State Parenting Act in the Courts." *Washington Law Review* 69 (1994): 679.

Emery, Robert. "Children in the Divorce Process." *Journal of Family Psychology* 2, no. 2 (1988): 141–144.

Engel, George, MD. "The Need for a New Medical Model: A Challenge for Biomedicine." *Science* 196 (1977): 129.

Epstein, Samuel, MD *Environmental Medicine*. New York University Child Study Center, 2005. http://www.nyu.edu/childstudy.

"Facts about Children and the Law—State Laws Regarding Joint Custody," Table 4, American Bar Association. http://www. abanet.org/media/ factbooks/cht4.html.

Family Law Changes to Alter Parenting. American Bar Association, 2006. http://www.abc.net.au/news/newsitems /200607/s 1676256.html (accessed 7 January 2006).

Farrell, Warren. *Father and Child Reunion*. New York: Jeremy Tarcher/Putnam, 2001.

Fassel, Diane. *Growing Up Divorced: A Road to Healing For Adult Children of Divorce*. New York: Pocket Books, 1991.

Fathers' Rights. N.O.W. Action Alert. Proceedings from National Conference Resolution, National Organization for Women. Washington, D.C., 1996. http://www.now-org/organization/ conference/ 1996/resolut:html (accessed 10 January 2006).

Fine, Mark, and Lawrence Kurdek. "Issues in Proposing a General Model of the Effects of Divorce on Children." *Journal of Marriage and Family* 55, no. 1 (1993): 31.

Fisher, Bruce, and Robert Alberti. *Rebuilding When Your Relationship Ends.* Atascadero, Ca.: Impact Publishers, 2000.

Florida State Statutes. Custody. Section 741.01–4, Subsection (5), 1998.

"For Richer or Poorer." *Mother Jones* 1 (2005): 8.

Fraser, Natalie. "The Consequences of Social and Family Dysfunction: A Perspective from New Zealand." *Trauma Response,* 1997.

Friedman, Debra. *Towards a Structure of Indifference: The Social Origins of Material Custody.* New York: Aldine de Gruyter, 1995.

Furstenberg, Frank F., and Christine W. Nord. "Parenting Apart: Patterns of Child Rearing after Marital Dissolution." *Journal of Marriage and the Family* 47 (1985): 894.

Garber, Benjamin D. "ADHD or Not ADHD: Custody and Visitation Considerations." *New Hampshire Bar News,* 9 February 2001.

Gardner, Richard, MD "Recent Trends in Divorce and Custody." *Litigation* 20, no. 3 (1985): 6.

_____. *The Parental Alienation Syndrome.* New Jersey: Creative Publishers, 1995.

Garrity, C. B., and M. A. Baris. *Caught in the Middle: Protecting Children of High Conflict Divorce.* New York: Lexington, 1994.

"George Engel Dies." *Currents* 28, no. 1 (January 2000): 1.

Grall, Timothy. "Custodial Mothers and Fathers and Their Child Support: 2001." *Current Population Reports* (October 2003).

Gray, John. *Men Are From Mars, Women Are From Venus.* New York: Harper Collins, 1992.

Gregory, John, et al. *Understanding Family Law.* New York: Matthew Bender and Company, 2001.

Grych, J., and F. Fincham. "Interviews of Children of Divorce: Toward Greater Integration of Research and Action." *Psychology Bulletin* 111, no. 3 (1992): 434–454.

Guidelines for Access and Visitation Center, 2003. Pamphlet describes guidelines for collaboration between New Haven Family Alliance Agency and the Southern Connecticut State University Family Clinic, New Haven, Conn., 2001.

Guidibaldi, John. "State of the States." *Speak Out for Children* 16 (2002): 12.

Gurian, Michael. *A Fine Young Man.* New York: Putnam, 1999.

Hartog, Hendrick. *Man and Wife in America.* Boston: Harvard College Press, 2000.

Hetherington, E. Mavis, and Margaret Stanley-Hagan. "The Adjustment of Children with Divorced Parents: A Risk and Resiliency Perspective." *Journal of Child Psychology and Psychiatry* 40, no. 1 (1999): 129–140.

Horn, Wade, remarks made at Center for Law and Social Policy, February 2004.

Huffer, Karin. *Overcoming the Devastation of Legal Abuse Syndrome.* Miami Florida: Fulkort Press, 1995.

"In the Matter of William Gregg, an Infant." *New York Legal Observer,* 1847, 266.

Interview with John Shonkoff. *CEA Advisor* 47, no. 7 (2005): 9.

Johnson, Janet R., and Linda E. G. Campbell. *Impasses of Divorce: The Dynamics and Resolution of Family Conflict.* New York: Free Press, 1988.

K. C. *Where's Daddy?* Richmond: Harbinger Press, 2002.

Kalter, Nell, and James Rembar. "The Significance of a Child's Age at the Time of Parental Divorce." *American Journal of Orthopsychiatry* 15, no. 1 (1981): 85.

Kay, Herma N. "Beyond No Fault: New Directions in Divorce Reform." *Divorce Reform at the Crossroads* 6, no. 36 (1990): 199.

Kelly, Joan B., and Judith S. Wallerstein. "Brief Interventions with Children in Divorcing Families." *American Journal of Orthopsychiatry* 47 no. 1 (January 1997): 27.

Klee, Brian, MD. *Changing the Face of Child Mental Health.* New York University Child Study Center, 2005. http://www.nyu.edu/ childstudy.

Klein, Rachel. "Are We Over-diagnosing ADHD in Our Kids?" New York Child Study Center, 2004. http://aboutourkids.org.

Knox, David, PhD. *The Divorced Dad's Survival Book.* New York: Plenum Press, 1998.

Krause, Harry D., ed. *Family Law,* 2nd ed. St. Paul, Minn.: West Publishing, 1996.

Krieder, Rose, and Jason M. Fields. "Number, Timing, and Duration of Marriages and Divorces: 1996." *U.S. Census Bureau Current Population Reports,* 2002.

Lamb, Michael E. *The Father's Role.* New York: Wylie and Sons, 1989.

Lansky, Vicki. *Divorce Book for Parents*. New York: New American Library, 1989.

Laws of Joint Custody. American Bar Association, 2001. http://www.helpyourselfdivorce.com/illinois-child-custody.html (accessed 2 April 2006).

Lee, Cheryl D. Custody Litigation. *Family and Conciliation Courts Review* 33, no. 3 (1995): 410.

Lee, Cheryl D., John L. Shaunessy, and Joel K. Bankes. "Impact of Expedited Visitation." *Family and Conciliation Courts Review* 33, 4 (1995): 495.

Lee, Margaret S., and Nancy W. Olesen. "Alienated Children in Divorce: Assessing for Alienation in Child Custody and Access Evaluations." *Family Court Review* 70 (2001): 282.

Levant, Ronald F. "Toward the Reconstruction of Masculinity." *Journal of Family Psychology* 5, no. 3 (1992): 92.

Leving, Jeffrey, J. D. *Fathers' Rights*. New York: Basic Books, 1997.

Levy, David L., ed. *The Best Parent Is Both Parents*. Norfolk: Hampton Roads, 1992.

_____. Editorial. *Children Magazine* 19, no. 1 (2004): 3.

_____. A Perspective of Joint Custody. *Children Magazine* (October 2005): 3.

Demosthenes Lorandos, William Bernet, S. Richard Sauber, *Parental Alienation: The Handbook for Mental Health and Legal Professionals*, 2nd ed. Charles C Thomas Pub Ltd, 2013.

Maccoby, Eleanor E., and Robert H. Mnookin. *Dividing the Child,* 2nd ed. Cambridge: Harvard University Press, 1997.

Maislin, Bonnie. *The Angry Marriage.* New York: Hyperion Press, 1994.

Maples, Mary Finn. "Consulting with the Judiciary: A Challenging Opportunity for the Counselor Educator." *The Eric Digest,* 1992.

Mason, Mary Ann. *The Custody Wars: Why Children Are Losing the Battles.* New York: Basic Books, 1999.

McGuire, Paula. *Putting It Together: Teenagers Talk about Family Breakups.* New York: Delacorte, 1987.

McKay, Dean, ed. "The Trauma of Divorce: Reducing the Impact of Separation on Children." *Trauma Response* 89(Summer 1998): 3.

McLanahan, Sarah. *Father Absence and the Welfare of Children.* Chicago, Il.: Network on the Family and the Economy. John D. and Catherine C. MacArthur Foundation, 2000. http://www.olin.wustl.edu/macarthur (accessed 4 October 2004).

McLanahan, Sarah, and Irv Garfinkle. "Fragile Families and Welfare Reform." *Children and Youth Services Review* 23, no. 4–5 (2001) 45.

McNeely, Cynthia. "Lagging Behind the Times: Parenting, Custody and Gender Bias in the Family Court." *Florida State University Law Review* 25 (1998): 956.

Melnhyk, Bernadette Mazurek, PhD, RN-CS, PNP, and Linda Alpert-Gillis, PhD. "Helping Parents and Children Cope with Divorce." *Advanced Practice Nursing Quarterly* 2, no. 4: 37.

Mercer, Diana, JD, and Marsha Kline Pruett, PhD. *Your Divorce Advisor.* New York: Fireside, 2001.

Mitchell, Anne. "The National Organization for Women Declares War on Fathers." *The Women's Freedom Network Newsletter* 4, no. 2 (1997): 18.

Morgan, Marni, and Marilyn Coleman. "Divorce and Adults." *Journal of the Cooperative Extension*. Columbia, Mo.: University of Missouri Press, 2001.

Neuman, M. Gary. *Helping Your Kids Cope with Divorce*. New York: Random House, 1998.

Nock, Steven. "Divorce Still Exacts Toll on U.S." *Speak Out for Children* 18 (2002): 17.

Novinson, Steven L. "Post-Divorce Visitation: Untying the Triangular Knot." *University of Illinois Law Review* 11, no. 1 (1983): 139.

Pagelow, Mildred. "Effects of Domestic Violence on Child Behavior and the Consequences for Custody and Visitation Agreements." *Mediation Quarterly* 7, no. 4 (Winter 1990): 437.

Paisley, Kay, and Sanford L. Braver. *Measuring Father Involvement in Divorced, Non-Resident Fathers*. Paper presented at annual meeting of the National Institute for Health, Bethesda, Md., 2001.

Paradise, Jo-Ellen. "The Disparity between Men and Women in Custody Disputes: Is Joint Custody the Answer to Everyone's Problems?" *St. John's Law Review* 72 (Spring 1998): 100.

Patient Rights. Accreditation Manual for Hospitals, Oakbrook Terrace, Il. Joint Commission on Accreditation of Healthcare Organizations, 1992.

Pearson, Jessica, and Nancy Thoennes. Resolving Issues of Access: Noncustodial Parents and Visitation Rights." *Public Welfare* 55, no. 4 (1997): 5.

Pedro-Carroll, Joanne. "The Promotion of Wellness in Children and Families." *American Psychologist* 998 (2001).

Pierce, LuAnn. *Growing Up Sane*. Tennessee: Jackson Publishing, 1997.

Popenoe, David. *Life Without Father* New York: Free Press, 1996.

"Preliminary Summary: Empirical Research Describing Outcomes of Joint Custody." American Psychological Association, 1995.

"Professor George Engel Dies." *Currents* 28, no. 1 (2000): 1.

"Re Marriage of La Musga," *12 Cal Rptr.* 32 Cal 4th 1072, 88P.3d 81 (2004): 356.

Reardon, John. *All-Star Dads*. Southington, Ct.: Glacier, 1997.

Rector, Robert E., Patrick F. Fagan, and Kirk A. Johnson. *Marriage: Still the Safest Place For Women and Children*. Washington, D.C., Office of Policy Research and Analysis, 2004. The Heritage Foundation. http://www.heritage.org/Research/Family/bg1732.cfm, (accessed 7 August 2005).

Red State vs. Blue State Divide. Wikipedia, http://en.wikipedia.org/wik/Red_states.html (accessed April 21 2006).

Remde, Harry. "Sadness in Art." *Parabola* 11, no. 3 (1986): 48.

Report on Governor's Commission of Divorce, Custody and Children. State of Connecticut Office of Policy Management, 2002.

Rohner, Ronald. *Annual Report, 3*. Storrs, Ct.: Rohner Center on Parental Acceptance and Rejection, 2003.

Rosenberg, Maxine B. *Living with a Single Parent*. New York: Bradbury, 1992.

Rural Income, Poverty, and Welfare: Rural Child Poverty. Washington, D.C.: U.S. Dept. of Agriculture, http:// ers.usda.gov/ briefing/ incomepovertywelfare/childpoverty.html (accessed 2 November 2005).

Saluter, Arlene F., and Terry A. Lugaila. "Marriage Status and Living Arrangements." U.S. Department of Commerce, Bureau of the Census, 1996.

Schwartz, Mary Ann, and Barbara Marliene Scott. *Marriages and Families, Diversity and Change* 4th ed. New York: Prentice Hall, 2003.

"Sharp Increase in Marriages of Teenagers Found in 90's." *New York Times*, 9 November 2002.

Sheehy, Gail. "The Divorced Dad's Burden." *New York Times*, 21 June 1998.

Sloan, Donna J. "Etiological Factors in the Emergence and Evolution of Alternative Medicine." *Alternative Medicine and Liberation Theology from 1960–2000* 2 (2003): 263.

Smith, George Edmond, MD, M.Ed. *More Than Sex: Reinventing The Black Male Image* New York: Kensington Books, 2000.

Stein, Laurie, and Shokofeh Dilmaghani. "Transitions: Meeting the Needs of Iranian Families Facing Separation and Divorce." *Family Service Association of Toronto Annual* (2002): 3.

Steinbreder, John, and Richard G. Kent, Esq. *Fighting For Your Life.* Dallas: Taylor Publishing Company, 1998.

Sullivan, Matthew, and Joan B. Kelly. "Legal and Psychological Management of Cases with an Alienated Child." *Family Court Review* 39, no. 3 (2001): 299.

Tesler, Pauline H. "Collaborative Law: A New Paradigm for Divorce Lawyers." *Psychology, Public Policy and Law* 5, no. 4 (1999): 967.

Theory of Ernst Haeckel. Berkeley: University of California, 1995, http://www.ucmp.berkeley.edu/history/haeckel.html (accessed 18 December 2005).

Turkat, Ira. "Parental Alienation Syndrome: A Review of Custody Issues." *Journal of the American Academy of Matrimonial Lawyers* 101, no. 18 (2002): 173.

U.S. Bureau of the Census, *Current Population Survey,* 1997.

U.S. Congress. House Committee on Healthy Children. Education, Labor and Pensions Subcommittee. Department of Health and Human Services. Washington, D.C., 2004

U.S. Department of Agriculture. *Rural Income, Poverty, and Welfare: Rural Child Poverty.* Washington, D.C., 2003. http:// ers. usda.gov/briefing/ incomepovertywelfare/childpoverty.html (accessed 3 March 2005).

U.S. Department of Health and Human Services. *HIPPA.* Washington, D.C., 2004. http://aspe.hhs.gov/HIPAAGenInfo// pl104191.html (accessed 12 December 2005).

U.S. Department of Health and Human Services. *Non-Custodial Parents' Participation in their Children's Lives: Evidence from the Survey of Income and Program Participation.* Washington, D.C.: Fatherhood Initiative, 1998.

U.S. Department of Justice. *Juvenile Female Crime: A Special Study,* Section V. Uniform Crime Reports for the United States, 1997.

U.S. Department of Justice. *Juvenile Offenders and Victims: 1999.* Washington, D.C. National Report Office of Juvenile Justice and Delinquency Prevention (3), 1999.

U.S. Department of Justice. *Juvenile Justice Bulletin*. Office of Juvenile Justice and Delinquency Prevention, 2002.

Von Durckheim, Graf, and Karl Fried. "Healing Power and Gesture." *Parabola* 30 (1986): 30.

Young, Cathy. *Ceasefire!* New York: The Free Press, 1999.

Waggenspack, Beth, ed. "The Search for Self-Sovereignty, Laws of 1860 c. 90, sec. 4." *Address to the New York State Legislature, 1860*. New York: Greenwood Press, 1989.

Wallace, Harvey. "Family Violence, Legal, Medical and Social Perspectives." San Francisco: Allyn and Bacon, 1999.

Wallerstein, Judith S., and Shauna B. Corbin. "Father-Child Relationships after Divorce: Child Support and Educational Opportunity." *Family Law Quarterly* 20, no. 4 (1986): 1140.

Wallerstein, Judith, and Joan Kelly. *Surviving the Breakup*. New York: Basic Books, 1996.

Wallerstein, Judith S., Julia M. Lewis, and Sandra Blakeslee. *The Unexpected Legacy of Divorce*. New York: Hyperion Press, 2000.

Ware, Ciji. *Sharing Parenthood after Divorce*. New York: Viking, 1982.

Wineburg, Howard, and James McCarthy. "Separation and Reconciliation in American Marriages." *Journal of Divorce and Remarriage* 20 (1993): 157.

Wolchik, Sharlene, et al. "Preventative Interventions for Children of Divorce." *JAMA* 288, no. 15 (1880).

ENDNOTE

1   Matthew Bramlett and William Mosher, "First Marriage Dissolution, Divorce, and Remarriage: United States," *Advance Data from Vital and Health Statistics* (May 2001): 323.

2   Arlene F. Saluter and Terry A. Lugaila, "Marriage Status and Living Arrangements" (Atlanta: U.S. Department of Commerce, Bureau of the Census, 1996): 48.

3   Timothy Grall, "Custodial Mothers and Fathers and their Child Support: 2001," *ion Reports*, October 2003, 1.

4   U.S. Bureau of the Census, "Child Custody," *Divorced Families, Current Population Survey*, 1997.

5   Ibid.

6   U.S. Bureau of the Census, *Cohabitation, Marriage and Divorce* 23, no. 22 (October 2003): 18.

7   Ibid.

8   Saluter and Lugaila op. cit., 3.

9   U.S. Department of Agriculture, *Rural Income, Poverty, and Welfare: Rural Child Poverty*, 3 March 2003, http://ers.usda.gov/briefing/incomepovertywelfare/childpoverty.

10   Mary Corcoran, "Nonresident Father Involvement and Child Well-Being: Can Dads Make a Difference?" *Journal of Family Issues* 15, no. 1 (March 1994): 96.

11   Rose Krieder and Jason M. Fields, "Number, Timing, and Duration of Marriages and Divorces, 1996," U.S. Bureau of the Census, *Current Population Reports* (February 2002), 18.

12   U.S. Bureau of the Census, *Cohabitation, Marriage, Divorce and Remarriage in the United States* 23, no. 22 (1998): 95.

13   Sarah McLanahan and Irv Garfinkle, "Fragile Families and Welfare Reform," *Children and Youth Services Review* 23, nos. 4–5 (2001): 45.

14   Vincent DiCaro, "With This Ring," *Fatherhood Today* 10, no. 3 (Summer 2005): 4–5.

15 "Sharp Increase in Marriages of Teenagers Found in 90s," *New York Times,* 9 November 2002.

16 Andrew Cherlin, *Divorce and Remarriage* (Cambridge: Harvard University Press, 1992), 89.

17 Bramlett, and Mosher, "Marriage Dissolution," 3.

18 George Edmond Smith, *More Than Sex: Reinventing the Black Male Image* (New York: Kensington Books, 2000), 166.

19 Howard Wineburg and James McCarthy, "Separation and Reconciliation in American Marriages," *Journal of Divorce and Remarriage* 20 (1993): 157.

20 Bramlett, and Mosher, "Marriage Dissolution," 4.

21 "For Richer or Poorer," *Mother Jones,* January/February 2005, 8.

22 "Red State vs. Blue State Divide," 2 February 2006, http://en.wikipedia.org/wik/Red_states.

23 Florida State Statutes, Section 741.01–4, Subsection (5).

24 Ronald F. Levant, "Toward the Reconstruction of Masculinity," *Journal of Family Psychology* 5, no. 3 (Fall 1992): 92.

25 Ibid., 42.

26 Natalie Fraser, "The Consequences of Social and Family Dysfunction: A Perspective from New Zealand," *Trauma Response,* 1997.

27 Mary Ann Mason, *The Custody Wars: Why Children Are Losing the Battles* (New York: Basic Books, 1999), 101.

28 Harry D. Krause, ed., *Family Law,* 2nd ed. (St. Paul, Minnesota: West Publishing, 1996), 199.

29 Debra, Friedman, *Towards a Structure of Indifference: The Social Origins of Material Custody* (New York: Aldine de Gruyter, 1995), 129.

30 Constance Ahrons and L. Wallisch, "Parenting in the Binuclear Family: Relationships between Biological and Stepparents," in K. Pasley and M. Ihinger-Tallman, eds., *Remarriage and Step Parenting: Current Research and Theory* (New York: Guilford Press, 1995), 256.

31 Sanford Braver and Diane O'Connell, *Divorced Dads: Shattering the Myths* (New York: Jeremy P. Tarcher, Division of Putnam, 1998), 224.

32 Ibid.

33 Robert Bauserman,. "Child Adjustment in Joint-Custody Versus Sole-Custody Arrangements: A Meta-Analytic Review." *Journal of Family Psychology* 16, no. 1 (2002): 91–102.

34 Ibid., 99.

35 James Atkinson, "Joint Custody Determination," *American Association Guide to Family Law,* 10 January 1996, http://ww.abanet.org/family/faq.htm.

36 Judy Dunn, et al., "Children's Relationships with their Nonresident Fathers," *Journal of Child and Adolescent Psychology* 45, no. 3 (March 2004): 566.

37 Jeffrey Leving, *Fathers' Rights* (New York: Basic Books, 1997), 57.

38   Karin Huffer, *Legal Abuse Syndrome* (Miami: Fulkort Press, 1995), 29.

39   Braver and O'Connell op.cit, 100.

40   "Laws of Joint Custody," 2 April 2001, http://helpyourselfdivorce.com Illinois-Child-Custody.html.

41   Ibid.

42   Ibid.

43   Herma N. Kay, "Beyond No Fault: New Directions in Divorce Reform," *Divorce Reform at the Crossroads* 6, no. 36 (New Haven: Yale University Press, 1990): 199.

44   Jo-Ellen Paradise, "The Disparity Between Men and Women in Custody Disputes: Is Joint Custody the Answer to Everyone's Problems?" *St. John's Law Review* 72 (Spring 1998): 100.

45   David Levy, interview by author, Hyattsville, Md., 28 June 2006.

46   Francesc Borrell-Carrio, Anthony L. Suchman, and Ronald Epstein, "The Biopsychosocial Model 25 Years Later: Principles, Practice, and Scientific Inquiry," *Annals of Family Medicine* 2, no. 6 (2004): 582.

47   Jessica Pearson and Nancy Thoennes, "Resolving Issues of Access: Noncustodial Parents and Visitation Rights," *Public Welfare* 55, no. 4 (Fall 1997): 5.

48   Braver and O'Connell op. cit., 173.

49   Steven Nock, "Divorce Still Exacts Toll on U.S.," *Speak Out for Children* 18, no. 2 (2002): 17.

50   Linda Wasmer Andrews, "Coping with Divorce," *HR Magazine* 50, no. 5 (May 2005): 61.

51   Ibid., 60.

52   Ibid., 61.

53   Eleanor Maccoby and Robert Mnookin, *Dividing the Child: Social and Legal Dilemmas of Custody,* 2nd ed. (Cambridge: Harvard University Press, 1997), 284-285

54   Braver and O'Connell op. cit., 49.

55   Gail Sheehy, "The Divorced Dad's Burden," *New York Times,* 21 June 1998.

56   William Doherty, Edward Koneski, and Martha Farrell Erickson, "Noncustodial Parents' Participation in their Children's Lives: Evidence from the Survey of Income and Program Participation," *Report from the Fatherhood Initiative* (1998), 25.

57   raver and O'Connell op. cit., 53.

58   Ibid., 218.

59   Gregory, John, et al., *Understanding Family Law* (New York: Mathew Bender and Company, July 2001), 15.

60　Jeffrey T. Cookston, Sanford L. Braver, Irwin Sandler, and M. Toni Genalo, "Prospects for Expanded Parent Education Services for Divorcing Families with Children," *Family Court Review* 40 (April 2002): 191.

61　Brenda L. Bacon and Brad McKenzie, "Parent Education after Separation/ Divorce: Impact of the Level of Parental Conflict on Outcomes," *Family Court Review* 42, no. 2 (January 2005): 263.

62　Susan Horwitz, interview by author, 2 February 2005, Rochester, N.Y.

63　James Atkinson, "Joint Custody Determination," *American Association Guide to Family Law,* 10 January 1996, http://ww.abanet.org/family/faq.htm.

64　Hendrick Hartog, *Man and Wife in America* (Boston: Harvard College Press, 2000), 210.

65　Ibid., 211.

66　Harry D. Krause, ed., *1996 Family Law,* 2nd ed. (St. Paul, Minn.: West Publishing Company, 1996), 199.

67　Ibid., 199.

68　Julie Artis, "Judging the Best Interests of the Child: Judges' Accounts of the Tender Years Doctrine," *Law Society Review* 38 (December 2004): 779.

69　Ibid., 789.

70　John Steinbreder and Richard G. Kent, *Fighting for Your Life* (Dallas: Taylor Publishing Company, 1998), 6.

71　Judith Wallerstein and Joan Kelly, *Surviving the Breakup* (New York: Basic Books, 1996), 136.

72　Maccoby and Mnookin op. cit., 284.

73　Jane W. Ellis, "Reconciling Discretion and Justice in Parenting Plan Disputes: The Washington State Parenting Act in the Courts," *Washington Law Review* 69 (1994): 679.

74　Maria Cancian and Daniel R. Meyer, "Who Gets Custody?" *Demography* 35, no. 2 (1998): 148.

75　Ibid., 157.

76　Robyn E. Blumner, "Court Ordered Sexism," *St. Petersburg Times,* 16 May 2004.

77　Artis, "Judging the Best Interests of the Child: Judges' Accounts of the Tender Years Doctrine," *Law Society Review* 38 (2004): 781.

78　David L. Levy, "A Perspective of Joint Custody," *Children Magazine,* October 2005, 3.

79　M. Gary Neuman, *Helping Your Kids Cope with Divorce* (New York: Random House, 1998), 6.

80　Janet Eaton, "Parenting Relationship after Divorce: Implications of Rationalization Regarding Well-being of Children" (PhD diss., The Union Institute, 1998).

81 Cheryl D. Lee, John Shaugessy, and Joel K. Bankes, "Impact of Expedited Visitation," *Family and Conciliation Courts Review* 33, no. 4 (October 1995): 495.

82 Constance Ahrons and Richard Miller, "The Effect of Post Divorce Relationship on Paternal Involvement: A Longitudinal Analysis," *American Journal of Orthopsychiatry* 63, no. 3:447.

83 Paul Amato and Cathryn Booth, "Children of Divorce in the 1990s," A *Journal of Family Psychology* 55 (September 2001): 357.

84 E. Mavis Hetherington and Margaret Stanley-Hagan, "The Adjustment of Children with Divorced Parents: A Risk and Resiliency Perspective," *Journal of Child Psychology and Psychiatry* 40, no. 1 (Winter 1999): 134.

85 Braver and O'Connell op. cit. 205

86 Ibid.

87 Ibid.

88 Matthew Sullivan and Joan B. Kelly, "Legal and Psychological Management of Cases with an Alienated Child," *Family Court Review* 39, no. 3 (Summer 2001): 299.

89 Mildred Pagelow, "Effects of Domestic Violence on Child Behavior and the Consequences for Custody and Visitation Agreements," *Mediation Quarterly* 7, no. 4 (Winter 1990): 437.

90 Laurie Stein and Shokofeh Dilmaghani, "Transitions: Meeting the Needs of Iranian Families Facing Separation and Divorce," *Family Service Association of Toronto Annual*, March 2002, 3.

91 Bernadette Mazurek Melnhyk and Linda Alpert-Gillis, "Building Healthier Families: Helping Parents and Children Cope with Divorce," *Advanced Practice Nursing Quarterly* 2, no. 4 (1997): 37.

92 Gregory, *Understanding Family Law,* 15.

93 Richard Gardner, "Recent Trends in Divorce and Custody," *Litigation* 20, no. 3 (1985): 6.

94 Ira Turkat, "Parental Alienation Syndrome: A Review of Custody Issues," *Journal of the American Academy of Matrimonial Lawyers* 101, no. 18 (2002): 173.

95 John Dunne and Marsha Hedrick, "The Parental Alienation Syndrome: An Analysis of Sixteen Selected Cases," *Journal of Divorce and Remarriage* 21, no 3/4 (1994): 27.

96 Ibid., 28.

97 Margaret S. Lee and Nancy W. Olesen, "Alienated Children in Divorce: Assessing for Alienation in Child Custody and Access Evaluation," *Family Court Review* 70 (July 2001): 284.

98 Bonnie Maislin, *The Angry Marriage* (New York: Hyperion Press, 1994), 178.

99 Karin Huffer, *Overcoming the Devastation of Legal Abuse Syndrome* (Miami, Fla.: Fulkort Press, 1995), 18.

100 Mark Fine and Lawrence Kurdek, "Issues in Proposing a General Model of the Effects of Divorce on Children," *Journal of Marriage and Family* 55, no. 1 (February 1993): 31.

101 Hetherington and Stanley-Hagen, "Adjustment of Children," 133.

102 Judith Wallerstein, Julia M. Lewis, and Sandra Blakeslee, *The Unexpected Legacy of Divorce* (New York: Hyperion Press, 2002), 311.

103 Amy J.L. Baker and Douglas Darnall, Behaviors and Strategies Employed in Parental Alienation, *"Journal of Divorce and Remarriage* (May 2006): 119

104 Dean McKay, "The Trauma of Divorce: Reducing the Impact of Separation on Children," *Trauma Response* (Summer 1998): 89. 3.

105 Lee and Olesen, "Alienated Children," 282.

106 Marni Morgan and Marily Coleman, "Divorce and Adults," *Journal of the Cooperative Extension* (October 2001): 2.

107 Ibid.

108 Mary Finn Maples, "Consulting with the Judiciary: A Challenging Opportunity for the Counselor Educator," *The Eric Digest* (December 1992): 101.

109 Kay Paisley and Sanford L. Braver, "Measuring Father Involvement in Divorced, Nonresident Fathers" (paper presented at the annual meeting of the National Institute for Health, Bethesda, Md., 3 March 2001.)

110 Joan B. Kelly and Judith S. Wallerstein, "Brief Interventions with Children in Divorcing Families," *American Journal of Orthopsychiatry* 47, no. 1 (January 1997): 27.

111 Ibid., 2.

112 Cynthia McNeely, "Lagging Behind the Times: Parenting, Custody, and Gender Bias in the Family Court," *Florida State University Law Review* 25 (1998): 956.

113 Sarah McLanahan, *Father Absence and the Welfare of Children* (Chicago: Network on the Family and the Economy, John D. and Catherine T. MacArthur Foundation, 2000), http://www.olin,wustl.edu/macarthur, 48.

114 Ibid.

115 Paul Amato and John Gilbreth, "Nonresident Fathers and Children's Well-Being: A Meta-Analysis," *Journal of Marriage and the Family* 61, no. 3 (August 1999): 557.

116 Joanne Pedro-Carroll, "The Promotion of Wellness in Children and Families," *American Psychologist* (November 2001): 998.

117 Ronald Rohner, *Annual Report* (Storrs, Conn.: Rohner Center on Parental Acceptance and Rejection, 2003), 3.

118 Ibid., 14.

119 Sarah McLanahan, *Father Absence and the Welfare of Children* (Chicago: Network on the Family and the Economy, John D. and Catherine T. MacArthur Foundation, 2000), http://www.olin,wustl.edu/macarthur, 48.

120 Michael Gurian, *A Fine Young Man* (New York: Putnam, 1999), 25.

121 U.S. Department of Justice, Office of Juvenile Justice and Delinquency Prevention, *Juvenile Justice Bulletin* (November 2002), 9.

122 U.S. Department of Justice, "Juvenile Female Crime: A Special Study, Section V.," *Uniform Crime Reports for the United States* (1997).

123 U.S. Department of Justice, Office of Juvenile Justice and Delinquency Prevention, "Juvenile Offenders and Victims, 1999," *National Report* (3).

124 Ibid., 18.

125 Nell Kalter and James Rembar, "The Significance of a Child's Age at the Time of Parental Divorce," *American Journal of Orthopsychiatry* 15, no. 1 (January 1981): 85.

126 McLanahan, *Father Absence*, 48.

127 Sharlene Wolchik, et al., eds., "Preventative Interventions for Children of Divorce," *Journal of the American Medical Association* 288, no. 15 (October 2002): 1880.

128 Kalter and Rembar, Op. Cit.

129 Amato and Gilbreth, "Nonresident Fathers," 377.

130 Rachel Klein, "Are We Over-Diagnosing ADHD in Our Kids?" January 2004, http://www.aboutourkids.org.

131 Nellie Filippopoulos, interview by author, 18 February 2006.

132 Ibid.

133 Benjamin D. Garber, "ADHD or Not ADHD: Custody and Visitation Considerations," *New Hampshire Bar News,* 9 February 2001, 51.

134 David A. Chiriboga and Linda S. Catron, *Divorce: Crisis, Challenge or Relief* (New York: New York University Press, 1991), 39.

135 Klein, "Are We Over-Diagnosing our Children?"

136 Ibid.

137 Samuel Epstein, "Environmental Medicine," New York University Child Study Center, www.nyu.edu/childstudy.

138 Brian Klee, "Changing the Face of Child Mental Health," 8 February 2005, *New York University Child Study Center,* www.nyu.edu/childstudy.html.

139 Kelly Zinna, interview by author, 18 December 2002.

140 Ibid., 94.

141 Interview with John Shonkoff, *CEA Advisor* 47, no. 7 (March 2005): 9.

142 "George Engel Dies," *Currents* 28, no. 1 (January 2000): 1.

143 Ibid., 2.

144 Fraser, *Consequences of Social and Family Dysfunction,* 189.

145 Borrell-Carrio, Francesca, Anthony L. Suchman, and Ronald Epstein, MD 2004. "Biopsychosocial Model 25 Years Later: Principles, Practice, and Scientific Inquiry," *Annals of Family Medicine* 2 (2004): 586.

146 Kovscek, Anastasia, interview by author, 15 June 2002.

147 George J. Cohen, "Helping Children and Families Deal with Divorce and Separation" *Pediatrics* 110, no. 6 (November 2002): 1019.

148 Borrell-Corrio, "Biopsychosocial Model," 586.

149 Pauline H. Tesler, "Collaborative Law: A New Paradigm for Divorce Lawyers," *Psychology, Public Policy and Law* 5, no. 4 (1999): 988.

150 Urie Bronfenbrenner, *The Ecology of Human Development* (Cambridge: Harvard University Press, 1979), 90.

151 Judith S. Wallerstein, Julia M. Lewis, and Sandra Blakeslee, *The Unexpected Legacy of Divorce* (New York: Hyperion Press, 2000), 311.

152 Larry L. Bumpass, James A. Sweet, and Andrew Cherlin, "The Role of Cohabitation in Declining Rates of Marriage," *Journal of Marriage and the Family* 53 (Winter 1991): 913.

153 Jeffrey Cottrill, "The State of the Union," *Divorce Magazine* 1, no. 3 (September, 2004): 60.

154 Braver and O'Connell, *Divorced Dads,* 52.

155 Bruce Fisher and Robert Alberti, "Rebuilding When Your Relationship Ends," 3rd ed. (Atascadero, Ca.: Impact Publishers, 2000), 18.

156 John Gray, *Men Are From Mars, Women Are From Venus* (New York: Harper Collins, 1992).

157 Smith op cit. *More than Sex,* 149.

158 Ibid.

159 Tesler, "Collaborative Law," 967.

160 Hartog, *Man and Wife,* 14.

161 Ibid., 14.

162 Ibid., 14.

163 Beth Waggenspack, ed., "The Search for Self-Sovereignty, Laws of 1860 c. 90, sec. 4," *Address to the New York State Legislature, 1860* (New York: Greenwood Press, 1989), 14.

164 Lucy Reyes, interview with author, 25 February 2002.

165 Rohner, *Annual Report,* 3.

166 Blong, Detzner, Keuster, Eliason, and Allan, "Developing Culturally Sensitive Parent Education Programs for Immigrant Families: The Helping Youth Succeed Curriculum," *Hmong Studies Journal* 5 (2006): 1–29.

167 Harvey Wallace, *Family Violence: Legal, Medical and Social Perspectives* (San Francisco: Allyn and Bacon, 1999), 184.

168 I urge the reader to question the presence of control when these signs appear.

169 Wallace, Family Violence, 186.

170 David Popenoe, *Life Without Father* (New York: Free Press, 1996), 218.

171 During litigation at New Haven Superior Court, 4 February 2003.

172 Statement noted by author at meeting of the Maryland Bar Association, 18 December 2002.

173 American Bar Association, "Facts About Children and the Law—State Laws Regarding Joint Custody," Table 4, www.abanet.org/media/factbooks/cht4.html.

174 "Re Marriage of La Musga," *12 Cal Rptr.* 32 Cal 4ᵗʰ 1072, 88P.3d 81 (2004): 356.

175 "La Musga," April 2004, California Women's Law Center, www.cwlc.org (accessed 4 October 2005).

176 "Re Marriage," 358.

177 Cynthia McNeely, "Lagging Behind the Times: Parenting, Custody and Gender Bias in the Family Court," *Florida State University Law Review* 25 (Summer, 1998): 956.

178 Blumner, Robyn. "Court-Ordered Sexism." *St. Petersburg Times.* 16 May 2004.

179 National Organization for Women, "Fathers' Rights," NOW Action Alert, now-org/organization/conference/1996/resolut:html (1996 proceedings from National Conference Resolution, accessed 10 January 2006).

180 Anne Mitchell, "The National Organization for Women Declares War on Fathers," *The Women's Freedom Network Newsletter* 4, no. 2 (Spring 1997): 18.

181 Steven L. Novinson, "Post-Divorce Visitation: Untying the Triangular Knot," *University of Illinois Law Review* (Spring 1983): 139.

182 Janice O'Donnell, interview with author, 8 March 2003. O'Donnell was liaison for collaboration between Providence Children's Museum and DCYF's "Families Together" Child Visitation program.

183 Judith S. Wallerstein and Shauna B. Corbin, "Father-Child Relationships after Divorce: Child Support and Educational Opportunity," *Family Law Quarterly* 20, no. 4 (Summer 1986): 1140.

184 Wade Horn, Center for Law and Social Policy, February 2004.

185 Sarah McLanahan and Irv Garfinkle, "Fragile Families and Welfare Reform," *Children and Youth Services Review* 23, no. 4–5 (2001): 45.

186 U.S. Bureau of the Census, *Marriage and Family Statistics* (1997): 18.

187 U.S. Bureau of the Census, *Current Population Survey,* 1997.

188 Maria Cancian and Daniel R. Meyer, "Who Gets Custody?" *Demography* 35, no. 2 (1998): 148.

189 David Levy, editorial, *Children Magazine* 19, no. 1 (Spring 2004): 3.

190 Jason Bradshaw and John Miller, "Lone Parent Families in the U.K.," *Her Majesty's Society of Orthopsychiatry* (London: HMSO, 1991): 18.

191 American Bar Association, "Family Law Changes to Alter Parenting," 7 January 2006, ABC News, http://www.abc.net.au/news/news/stories/2006/07/0/1676256.htm.

192 Jack Greenberg, interview, *Fresh Air* (radio program), National Public Radio, 15 May 2004.

193 Ibid.

194 Jeanne H. Block, Jack Block, and Per. F. Gjerde, "The Personality of Children Prior to Divorce," *Child Development* 57 (August 1986): 827.

195 Leo Buscaglia, *Living, Loving and Learning* (New York: Ballentine Books, 1983), 93.

196 Ibid., 94.

197 "Creed of Healing," The Reiki Plus Institute of Natural Healing, www.reikiplus.com/new.html (accessed 9 February 2005).

198 George Engel, "The Need for a New Medical Model: A Challenge for Biomedicine," *Science* 196 (1977): 129.

199 Barbara Gaydos, "Creativity and Spirituality: Toward a Matriarchal Aesthetic" (lecture, 24 July 2000, Santa Fe, N.M.).

200 Barbara Montgomery Dossey, "Creativity and Spirituality: Toward a Matriarchal Aesthetic" (lecture, 25 July 2000, Santa Fe, N.M.).

201 Barbara Dossey, ed. *Holistic Nursing, A Handbook for Practice,* 3rd ed. (Aspen: Aspen Publishers, 2000), 8.

202 Ibid., 9.

203 "Patient Rights," *Accreditation Manual for Hospitals* (Oakbrook Terrace, Ill.: Joint Commission on Accreditation of Healthcare Organizations, 1992), 263.

204 Donna J. Sloan, "Etiological Factors in the Emergence and Evolution of Alternative Medicine," *Alternative Medicine and Liberation Theology from 1960–2000* (June 2003): 263.

205 Patricia Bird, interview with author, 5 April 2004.

206 Ibid.

207 "HIPPA," 1 December 1997, http://aspe.hhs.gov/HIPAAGenInfo/pl104191.htm.

208 "Best Interest of the Child Standard in Connecticut," 6 December 2005, www.jud.ct.gov/ lawlib/notebooks/pathfinders/BestInterestsoftheChildStandard/BestInterest.htm.

209 Braver and O'Connell, op. cit. 53.

210 Future of Parent Education, Connecticut Supreme Court, Hartford, Conn., 8 May 2004.

211 Maples, Mary Finn. "Consulting with the Judiciary: A Challenging Opportunity for the Counselor Educator." *The Eric Digest*, 1992., 103.

212 Wallerstein, Lewis, and Blakeslee, *Unexpected Legacy*, 311.

213 "An Overview of Florida's Criminal Justice Specialized Courts," *Florida Community Commission Report* 97 (October 1997): 231.

214 Connecticut Office of Policy Management, "Report on Governor's Commission of Divorce, Custody and Children" (February 2002).

215 *Guidelines for Access and Visitation Center* (2003), 4. Pamphlet describes guidelines for collaboration between New Haven Family Alliance Agency and the Southern Connecticut State University Family Clinic, New Haven, Conn., 2001.

216 Ibid, 174

217 O'Donnell, interview by author, October 18, 2001.

218 Frank F. Furstenberg and Christine W. Nord, "Parenting Apart: Patterns of Child Rearing after Marital Dissolution," *Journal of Marriage and the Family* 47 (November 1985): 894.

219 Buscaglia, "Don't Be Fooled By Me," 18.

220 Ibid.

221 "Theory of Ernst Haeckel," www.ucmp.berkeley.edu/history/haeckel.html.

222 Menninger, Karl Quote, p. 181

223 David Gray Ross, presentation, First National Child Access/Safe Haven Training Conference, 4 October 2002, Hanover, Md.

224 Diana Mercer and Marsha Kline Pruett, *Your Divorce Advisor* (New York: Fireside, 2001).

225 Ibid., 18.

226 Harry Remde, "Sadness in Art," *Parabola* 11, no. 3 (Fall 1986): 48.

227 Sidney Roseman, 1 May 1997.

228 Joy Berger, unpublished manuscript, "The Four Cornerstones of Healing," June 2003, 14.

229 Ibid., 14.

230 Hillary Clinton, "Remarks at the Democratic National Convention," *Associated Press,* 27 August 1996.

231 Judith Wallerstein, interview with author, Mill Valley, Ca., 9 January 2001.

232 Justice Brandeis Quote.

233 Thomas F. Babor, John C. Higgins-Biddle, Pamela S. Higgins, Ruth A. Gassman, and Bruce E. Gould, "Training Medical Providers to Conduct Alcohol Screening and Brief Interventions," *Substance Abuse* 25, no. 1 (2004): 24.

234 Darnall Douglas, *Divorce Casualties, Protecting Your Children from Parental Alienation* (Dallas: Taylor Publishing Company, 1998).

235 Ibid., 63.

236 Ibid., 65.

237 Braver and O'Connell op. cit., 207.

238 Eleanor Maccoby and Robert Mnookin, *Dividing the Child,* 2nd ed. (Cambridge: Harvard University Press, 1992), 287.

239 Ibid., 291.

240 Paisley and Braver, "Measuring Father Involvement."

241 Cheryl D. Lee, John L. Shaunessy, and Joel K. Bankes, "Impact of Expedited Visitation," *Family and Conciliation Courts Review* 33, 4 (October 1995): 495.

242 John Guidibaldi, "State of the States," *Speak Out for Children* 16 (May 2002): 12.

243 Cancian and Meyer, "Who Gets Custody?"149.

244 *Laws of Joint Custody*, Chicago, Ill.: American Bar Association, 2001, http://www.helpyourselfdivorce.com/illinois-child-custody.html (accessed 2 April 2006).

PART III

THE CHILD CUSTODY JOURNEY

Section 1

Legislative Achievements for Child Custody

Advocacy and Education

Legislative Achievements for Child Custody

Background

The attached photographs share a common thread, efforts by individuals, together, to create improved outcomes for children by examining public policy and state statutes, and sharing the research on shared parenting at public and professional forums.

Motivated by child access or child custody awards, which had been seemingly prejudiced towards mothers prior to 2000, parents sought to explore the court process and increasing social research to support the cause for joint custody. The research documented in this Handbook served to support the valuable consideration that both parents play a continuing role in parenting their children.

These social struggles characterized by demonstrations, presentations, and professional psychological testimony in the court room have resulted in increased court orders for shared parenting. These decisions then have been a catalyst for increasing social research and professional witnesses appearing before state legislatures to affect major modifications in family law child custody statutes of more than thirty states.

The author participated in many of the aforementioned tactics in metropolitan DC and New England to galvanize local support for these statue changes. I encountered as much reception and support for joint custody in the general populace as there had been opposition from the professional organizations and rigid legislatures. State legislatures became more receptive over time, particularly as the Children's Rights Council published the social research, and shared it through annual conferences, legislative testimony, presentations to Bar Associations, public speaking.

Today, advocacy remains a significant means to bring joint custody education to those few states without such family protections, including Michigan, Maryland and Massachusetts. Several of these organizations which continue to lobby and educate the legislatures of their states include Nate Holstein's National Parent Organization in

Boston, Massachusetts, Dads and Moms of Michigan, both founded in 1998, and the Children's Rights Fund founded in 2011 by David W. Smith, Sr. and David L. Levy, Esq., co-founder and former President of the Children's Rights Council in 1985.

Significant, too, have been the importance by child custody organizations, attorneys and universities demonstrating that increased use of family mediation and 'collaborative divorce' are sensible alternatives to financially costly and emotionally damaging litigation.

The late David L. Levy, Esq., co-founded the Children's Rights Council in Washington DC (1985) and spearheaded the joint custody movement in the US. Among his many honors, Rodale Press' Child Health Magazine named Levy in 2009 as "one of the top 25 people to help child outcomes in the last 50 years." Levy has been labeled the "King of Joint Custody" by Dr. Richard Sauber. Until his passing in 2014, Levy was the international 'face of joint custody', honored by the Ambassadors of France and the United Kingdom for his leading role in advocating national policies for shared parenting in these countries.

Supreme Court Justice Ruth Bader Ginsburg (center) is flanked by David Levy (right) and David W. Smith, Jr. (left) during one of Dave Levy's frequent visits to Judge Ginsburg's office. Levy frequently quoted Judge Ginsburg, who advocated that women's liberation would succeed as long as men were treated equally and fairly. A shared or co-parenting advocate, Levy frequently quoted Ginsburg's her statement, "*Women will only have true equality when men share with them the responsibility of bringing up the next generation.*" In 1997, First Lady Hillary Rodham Clinton honored David Levy's "outstanding contributions toward child advocacy" and awarded him the Legislative Achievement award in behalf of the child advocacy work of Children's Rights Council.

Maryland Governor Parris Glendenning (center) signing Senate Bill 63 (April 8, 1997) giving Maryland's circuit courts authority to require divorcing parents a) at least two hours of mediation to voluntarily resolve their child custody disputes, and b) attendance at a parenting class on the impact of divorce on children. Senate Bill 63was was proposed by CRC's David Levy, Esq. and introduced by Teresa Kaiser, Esq., Maryland Director of Child Support Enforcement (center, back row). To Kaiser's right is CRC national consultant, Dr. Harvey Walden, with Mary and Alfred Ellis, Director of Child Access Services. Al was a pioneer in supervised visitation, managing nearly forty CRC locations nationally.

House Bill 687 on Child Custody Decision Making, signed into law by Maryland Governor (and former Presidential Candidate) Martin O'Malley in May, 2014. David L. Levy, Esq. (center) contributed significantly to the Bill, with Maryland State Delegate Jill A. Carter (to left of David) the bill's co-sponsor. House Bill 687 formally established the Commission on Child Custody Decision Making which created an interdisciplinary professional and academic team approach to study child custody cases, their processes and outcomes, to review the literature in order to determine the feasibility for State of Maryland statutes on joint custody. David W. Smith, President of the Children's Rights Fund is to the left of State Delegate Carter.

David W. Smith, Sr. (2nd from left), President of the Children's Rights Fund (CRF) at the Maryland State Capitol, meeting with senior legislators and organization leaders advocating for shared parenting (2016). Smith is flanked on left by CRF Chief of Staff David Grogan, and on his right by Joe Jones, Executive Director of Center of Urban Families, Maryland Delegate Jill P. Carter, Dr. Franklyn Malone, CEO of the 100 Fathers, Inc., educator Tammy Foyles, community leader Nick Charles with his son. Both Malone and Jones are nationally leaders in advocating for low income parents. Jones has served as a consultant for federal and municipal policy affecting fathers and families.

The author (center) with microphone, speaking at the Parental Alienation Awareness Conference sponsored by Kids Need Both in Lakeland, Florida (2012). The panel of experts discussed dynamics in high conflict divorce, the use of psychological assessments in hearings, the value and therapeutic techniques for treating Parental Alienation, and court ordered interventions to reduce harmful brainwashing of children.

Section 2

Holistic Concepts for Family Healing
Multiple Services for Families Journeying
Through Divorce and Child Custody

Section 2

Holistic Concepts for Family Healing
Multiple Services for Families Journeying
Through Divorce and Child Custody

The Toby Center for Family Transitions

Background

Founded in 2008 and named in memory of the author's mother, The Toby Center for Family Transitions, Inc. is a service model for a one stop regional source for delivery of social services to improve child access when parents separate and divorce.

Each Center provides supervised visitation, family mediation, individual and family therapy, and peer support groups. The rationale for this concept is that family professionals (FP's) from different disciplines who can work together when serving the same, frequently traumatized population will have a far greater success rate for families in treatment. Center locations bring familiarity, resources, and therefore comfort to children and parents needing visitation, counseling, co-parenting education, and peer support.

The model is designed for replication in any metropolitan area where family courts are overwhelmed by frequently returning cases, where supervised visitation and related child access services are missing, and where integral therapeutic interventions and service uniformity is found lacking.

Impetus and Inspiration. Theodora Tobia 'Toby' Roseman, the author's mother provided the inspiration for the Toby Center. One of seven children, Toby grew up in Hartford, Connecticut and worked evenings after high school as a 'Rosie the Riveter' during WWII. When her children were fulltime in public school, Toby served as an assistant mental health instructor. An active proponent of civil rights in the turbulent 1960's, she taught her children about discrimination and racial abuse. During the Depression, she grew up across the street from her good friend, comedian Totie Fields and her cousin, TV impresario George Kirgo (nee Blumenthal). "Those were the days," she frequently told her son, Dr. Roseman, seated. "Family and friends are worth a million. Treat them all with loving kindness."

The first Toby Center (2010, Boynton Beach, Florida) The Toby Center was created by the author as a single provider of multiple services for parents and children seeking child custody determinations. Its corporate vision is to expand to other states where these services are in need. Dr. Roseman (third from left is pictured with the original Toby Center staff members, supporters and Florida Legislators. Rabbi Barry Silver, Esq., (center) has vociferously expounded on the virtues of parenting, and the need for court litigation to become more protecting a child's right to both parents. To Silver's right, is Kim Spavrum Ortiz, MS in Forensic Psychology, Guardian Ad Litem and U.S. Army Veteran who served as Toby Center's first General Manager. Palm Beach County Commissioner Steve Abrams is to right of Kim.

The Toby Center in 2017, with new staff serving families in twenty primary locations in South and Central Florida. (Front Row, l to r) Symantha Duncan, Assistant Regional Visitation Coordinator, Meredith Schlegel, Director of Toby Center Administration, Judy Kraft, lead therapist for South Florida, Vicki St. Sauveur, first visitation monitor for Central Florida, Thien Nguyen, Field Monitor. (Back row, second from left, Paula Duncan, Regional Visitation Coordinator, Polk County.

Toby Center logo – Designed in 2011 by former Toby Center intern from Lynn University, Stephanie Gowdy. The logo was adapted from a lithograph donated by Dr. Richard Sauber and titled "The Family" by Philadelphia Holocaust artist Gladys Sauber, mother of Dr. Sauber. When presented, Dr. Sauber stated, "I carefully selected this lithograph for you and it would be nice that both of our mothers combine their talents."

Toby Center trainings for Supervised visitation are based on the pioneering work of Alfred 'Al' Ellis, Children's Rights Council (CRC) Director of Child Access Services. Here, Al was training new staff at St. John's Episcopal Church in Bala Cynwyd, Pennsylvania in Greater Philadelphia (2006). Courts in many parts of the country had wanted to replicate the CRC supervised visitation program so Al with David Levy expanded CRC's supervised visitation program to be the largest provider of such services in the United States. Not only characterized by his slow, Southern gentlemanly drawl, Al was respected for his wisdom, kindness, sincere empathy, and special respect for children and both their parents, all suffering when parents separated.

South Florida Science Center and Aquarium, West Palm Beach, Florida. Children's museums offer children opportunities for creative interaction using visual, tactile and other learning activities and stimulating displays. Museums and parks challenge children to play, to explore, to learn about themselves, and to appreciate both parents for enabling such enjoyable experiences.

Shared Parenting Classroom, Family Fundamentals, Lakeland, Florida. In this classroom a young child enjoys a book with her mother. A community organization program supported by the Polk County United Way and Publix Supermarkets, Family Fundamentals occupies a former elementary school where many regional nonprofit agencies as the Toby Center can utilize these family friendly facilities.

Barnett Family Park, Lakeland, Florida. Parks are a frequent venue for Toby Center's supervised parenting time. For many young children and their parents, parks are family friendly locations which facilitate a fun, comfortable normalization of parent and child relationships.

Toby Center Hillsborough County Family Monitors (left and right) Miyunta Brown and Thien Nguyen meeting with Yaridis Garcia (center), Community Planning Manager for the Juvenile Welfare Board of Pinellas County. Networking within the region helped introduce the Toby Center services and to expand our services to Pinellas County in Central Florida. The JWB is the first Children's Services Council in Florida and helps municipal, private, nonprofit and the faith based community to collaborate in child focused services. Miyunta and Thien found their field work to be inspirational, and both subsequently enrolled in schools of mental health counseling

New Toby Center clinical and non clinical staff members celebrating the completion of their classroom training (2016). Judy Kraft (on left) is lead therapist for the Toby Center in Palm Beach County. The enthusiasm and camaraderie evidenced here is what parents do not find in the courthouse. Sensitivity and compassion are arguably two characteristics to most effectively help families heal from trauma of separation. Trained providers who offer supportive and clinical visitation provide the pathways for child and parent reunification, which research confirms create better outcomes for children.

Toby Center Service Areas and Offices*
Percentage of Families Who Could Not Afford Services

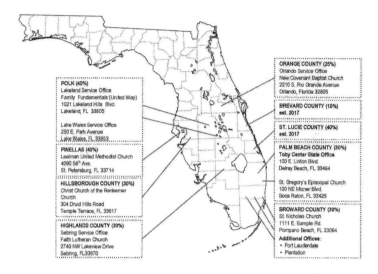

POLK (40%)
Lakeland Service Office
Family Fundamentals (United Way)
1021 Lakeland Hills Blvd.
Lakeland, FL 33805

Lake Wales Service Office
250 E. Park Avenue
Lake Wales, FL 33853

PINELLAS (40%)
Lealman United Methodist Church
4090 58th Ave.
St. Petersburg, FL 33714

HILLSBOROUGH COUNTY (30%)
Christ Church of the Redeemer
Church
304 Druid Hills Road
Temple Terrace, FL 33617

HIGHLANDS COUNTY (30%)
Sebring Service Office
Faith Lutheran Church
2740 NW Lakeview Drive
Sebring, FL33870

ORANGE COUNTY (25%)
Orlando Service Office
New Covenant Baptist Church
2210 S. Rio Grande Avenue
Orlando, Florida 32805

BREVARD COUNTY (10%)
est. 2017

ST. LUCIE COUNTY (40%)
est. 2017

PALM BEACH COUNTY (30%)
Toby Center State Office
100 E. Linton Blvd.
Delray Beach, FL 39484

St. Gregory's Episcopal Church
100 NE Mizner Blvd.
Boca Raton, FL 33429

BROWARD COUNTY (30%)
St. Nicholas Church
1111 E. Sample Rd.
Pompano Beach, FL 33064

Additional Offices:
• Fort Lauderdale
• Plantation

* Identified above are the Toby Center 'Primary Regional Locations' where staff hold initial meetings with client families. Here staff conduct client intakes and also begin therapy and visitation services. Client goals to reunify children in foster care with their biological parents and to supervise parenting time for child custody cases have staff most frequently select more family friendly locations and activities as museums, parks, restaurants, theater.

Updated November 2017

The Toby Center service area (as of Spring, 2017) finds that over 30% of parents calling the Toby Center cannot afford fees for supervised visitation, therapy and reunification services. When one considers that households earn much less when parents separate, then it is easier to understand why many parents cannot afford to see their children, even when permitted by court order. Funding for supervised visitation and family therapy is significantly lacking in many states, including Florida, the Toby Center's home state. The Federal Child Access and Visitation Block Grant first advocated by David Levy in the 1990's does provide money for these services to each state and based on population size. These funds are further allocated by each state to service providers. Historically in Florida, however, the Department of Children and Families has been the only recipient of these funds which are allocated solely for reunification of children in foster care.Thus, then is little money for family courts to allow for children whose families are seeking custody arrangements, therapy and family mediation which can improve child outcomes when parents separate.

Section 3

The Author's Journey

Acknowledgement, Recognition and Support

Section 3

The Author's Journey

Acknowledgement, Recognition and Support

The author has found support groups vital for those enduring trauma and related life transitions. In spite of one's level of confidence, no one can be expected to have all or most answers to assist themselves in navigating their divorce and child custody proceedings.

With acknowledgement of one's current and evolving family status, the individual can better address the options for achieving a more secure outcome. It is with the recognition that the legal and social processes now unfolding will likely be confusing and complicated, but not necessarily arduous. These processes will be costly, though not indefinite.

This period of one's life may then pass more comfortably through regular and accessible self care, and peer support.

David Levy believed this to be so true, for he regularly reminded staff and volunteers answering the Children's Rights Council Hotline to urge every person calling be directed to join a support group, or to start one.

The Ex Files is an article which described the significance of For Men Only, a men's divorce support group in Guilford, Connecticut where the author was a member (*Mirabella Magazine*, April 2000). It documented the many views of (then) recently separated and divorced men in the late 1990's. That Mirabella, a nationally prominent woman's magazine, had published this story of divorced men seeking support signified an historic turning point. It was the first significant and national recognition that fathers should, and could, be heard. The men featured in *The Ex Files* comprised an important support group through which, though feeling sad, frustrated, and angry, individuals from across socioeconomic strata could adjust to their divorce. It was through this common experience that male bonding was easier and most valuable. Founded by Dr. James 'Jim' Abrahams, lower left, this support group continues, having proved that well structured introspective and intimate discussion, and social activities can build valuable friendships at a time when many need validation, comfort, guidance and inclusion in a most lonely existence when divorce occurs. The author is on top, right.

ABOUT THE AUTHOR

Dr. Roseman is a divorced dad of three and founder and CEO of the Toby Center for Family Transitions, a comprehensive family service agency based in Florida and centered around the needs of families when parents choose to separate. The Toby Center genesis began during Roseman's doctoral research and confirmed by his work with single, separated, divorced and never married parents. He found child outcomes are maximized when multiple social, therapeutic and court services can be provided through a wraparound service delivery mode.

A Certified Family Life Educator, and Family Court Mediator, Dr. Roseman has worked with children and parents since 1998 when he became an advocate for joint custody. He worked closely with David L. Levy, Esq., co-founder and then President of the Children's Rights Council (CRC) in Washington, DC. From 2002 to 2008, Roseman served as Assistant Director for Child Access Services for the CRC developing curriculum and training for the CRC national supervised visitation program.

Roseman frequently quotes America's foremost pioneer in child psychiatry, Dr. Karl Menninger who stated that "What children see at home, they will do to society." With that philosophy in mind, he created The Toby Center with a focus that assisting parents to be more confident and satisfied will then their children will have a better opportunity to thrive.

Roseman is a motivational speaker, and specialist on high conflict divorce, parental alienation, and co-parenting. He is a contributor to the Huffington Post Online, and is a former columnist for Knight Ridder Tribune (2002-2005) where his column, Family Matters was published in 400 newspapers. He believes that we have opportunity to break through trauma when we can find validation, and humor.

He earned his Ph.D. in Family Studies from the Union Institute & University.